WRITERS AND READERS.

WRITERS AND READERS

BY

GEORGE BIRKBECK HILL

" Dreams, books, are each a world ; and books we know
Are a substantial world both pure and good."

Wordsworth

Essay Index Reprint Series

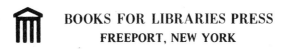

BOOKS FOR LIBRARIES PRESS
FREEPORT, NEW YORK

First Published 1892
Reprinted 1972

Library of Congress Cataloging in Publication Data

Hill, George Birkbeck Norman, 1835-1903.
 Writers and readers.

 (Essay index reprint series)
 Lectures read before members of the Teachers' University Association in residence at Oxford in 1891.
 1. English literature--History and criticism.
2. Literature--Study and teaching. I. Title.
PR99.H5 1972   820'.9   72-8517
ISBN 0-8369-7317-8

PREFACE.

———◇———

THE lectures which form this little work were read in the Hall of New College, before the members of the Teachers' University Association, who were in residence in Oxford during part of the Long Vacation of 1891.

CONTENTS.

LECTURE I.

LECTURE I.

I AM often amused by the confident air with which not only chance readers, but even students of literature appoint, as it were, the books which are to be the delight of posterity. Posterity, it has been well said, is the author's friend. The writer who cannot catch the ear of his own public pleases himself with the thought that his voice will be prolonged by the echoes of time, and will sound the more loudly the farther it has to travel. Southey, who with all his great merits as an ardent and thorough student, is scarcely known to the present generation but by one or two ballads and one biography, was supported through the neglect which his works encountered by the confident belief that posterity would do him justice. He talks in one place "of exposing the real character and history of the Romish Church, systematically and irrefragably, which (he says) I can and will do, in books which will be read now and hereafter ; which must make a part hereafter of every historical library, and which will live and act when I am gone." Speaking of the need under which he had always lived of gaining his livelihood by the pen, he says : " Under more favourable circumstances I might have accomplished more and better things. But when the grave-digger has put me to bed and covered me up, it will not be long before it will be perceived and acknowledged that there are few who have done so much." Of his poem of "Madoc" he writes : " Unquestionably the poem will stand and flourish. . . . William Taylor has said it is the best English poem that has left the press since the ' Paradise Lost' ; indeed this is not exaggerated praise, for unfortunately there is no competition." His " History of Brazil," he prophecies, " will ages hence be found among those works which are not destined to perish ; it will secure for me a remembrance in other countries as well as in my own ; it will be to the Brazilians what the work of Herodotus is to Europe." [1]

Who can be churlish enough to grudge to an honest worker, one of the most laborious authors

[1] Southey's " Life and Correspondence," ed. 1850, ii. 359 ; iv. 354 ; v. 274, 321.

that the world has ever seen, the comfort which he found for the neglect under which he was suffering? His books, it is true, were encumbering his publisher's warehouse. What of that? He appealed to future generations, to those happy times when the bubbles shall have burst which are raised in the vast whirlpools of fashion, and the bark of the poet and the historian, clear of the froth, shall be seen floating securely and quietly and triumphantly down the stream of time. Had he been of a less hopeful mind he might have got chilled by the words with which the learned Porson ends his Preface to his famous "Letters to Archdeacon Travis": "Mr. Travis and I may address our letters to posterity, but they will never be delivered according to the direction." Astronomers tell us that the nearest fixed star is at so vast a distance from us that, in spite of the incredible rapidity with which light travels, all we can know for certain is that it was shining at the time of the birth of a man of middle age. There are other stars so remote that we cannot feel sure that they did not fall with Julius Cæsar, when men were scared by seeing

"The strange impatience of the heavens."

Were a new constellation formed to-day at some

comparatively moderate distance, its light would perhaps first strike upon the world when the grandchild of the youngest person here present was falling into his dotage. Not a few of our literary luminaries, if we are to trust what they say of themselves and what is said of them, are in somewhat the same case. Their light has not yet reached us, the denseness through which it has to travel having much the same effect as space; but it will strike upon our descendants. No heart surely can be so hard as to refuse to a disappointed author his islands of the blest, on the other side, not of the western waves, but of the centuries. But the case is altogether different when pity no longer operates, when every reader presumes to settle who they are who are to be welcomed on those happy shores "with the sound of bells and acclamations of the people." What is freely allowed to compassion must not be conceded to ignorance and conceit. The taste of one generation is not to be fixed by the taste of another. We may give our favourite authors all the immortality we please. We may refuse to believe that an age can ever come so lost to good taste as to decline to admire those who are our delight. In matters of taste each age will judge for itself, and our descendants, if they examine into our judgments and our prophecies, will certainly obtain from them some amusement, but perhaps very little profit, unless they take the trouble to investigate the causes that rendered them so faulty.

Nevertheless, with how confident an air do we hear maintained what shall be the reading, not only of the next, but even of succeeding centuries. The guardian angels seem almost to be heard chanting, not only that Britons never shall be slaves, but that they never shall cease to be readers of Macaulay or Carlyle, of Herbert Spencer or Ruskin, of Browning or of George Eliot. Nay, there are minor stars, whose names I but imperfectly retain in my memory, who are to shine with increasing splendour for many a long day yet. No great while ago I heard in this University of Oxford a learned man maintain that a certain novelist, whose works I had never even glanced at, and whose name I have now forgotten, will be read five hundred years hence. When, as sometimes happens, my opinion is demanded, when I am asked whether this favourite author and that favourite author will not be the delight of our grandchildren and our great-grandchildren, I never venture to go beyond a negative kind of prophecy. I have little difficulty in coming to a decision as to those who will not be read ; but no prudent man,

who sees names which once filled everybody's
mouth now scarce known to the student, who sees
books which were once the pride of every library
now on some huckster's stall, labelled " All in this
lot at a penny a volume," will venture to foretell
immortality, or even a long duration of popularity,
to any work whatsoever of his own day. In matters of taste there is only one sure judge, and that
is time. "About things," says Johnson, "on which
the public thinks long it commonly attains to
think right." It is not one or two, perhaps not
even three generations which can arrive at a final
judgment of a work. The vast majority even of
those books which make a great noise are forgotten long before the third generation is reached ;
but the works of men of real genius require at least
the greater part of a century before their value can
be accurately ascertained. At first by their very
originality they often excite anger and even
contempt, running as they do against the fashion
of the day. Before they can get justice done them
they must establish a school of their own; but
their scholars are apt to pass into worshippers.
The neglect which they at first encountered gives
way to extravagant admiration ; they are rendered
ridiculous by their servile imitators ; a reaction
sets in, and once more they are placed below their

just level. Then there begins a fresh reaction in
their favour, till the balance which has swung now
too much up, and now too much down, settles at
last, and marks their real weight. There is a
passage in Johnson's " Life of Gray " which, I have
always thought, illustrates the career of the poet
who strikes into fresh paths. " In 1757," he writes,
" Gray published 'The Progress of Poetry' and
'The Bard,' two compositions at which the readers
of poetry were at first content to gaze in mute
amazement. Some that tried them confessed their
inability to understand them, though Warburton
said that they were understood as well as the
works of Milton and Shakespeare, which it is the
fashion to admire. Garrick wrote a few lines in
their praise. Some hardy champions undertook
to rescue them from neglect, and in a short time
many were content to be shown beauties which
they could not see."

Of how many poets whom we of this age admire
might the same be said! At the compositions
of Wordsworth, of Tennyson, of Browning, "the
readers of poetry were at first content to gaze
in mute amazement." Many who tried them either
could not understand them, or thought that there
was nothing in them to understand. Champions
soon arose; the difficulty experienced in discover-

ing their merits, when overcome, became a source
of pride ; and of those who remained blind, "many
were content to be shown beauties which they
could not see."

Jeffrey, the great Edinburgh reviewer, had treated
Wordsworth with a contempt that was almost
gross in its violence. His "Lyrical Ballads" he
"looked upon in a good degree as poetical
paradoxes—maintained experimentally, in order
to display talent and court notoriety ; and so
maintained with no more serious belief in their
truth than is usually generated by an ingenious
and animated defence of other paradoxes." [1]
Jeffrey was no common man ; in him there was
no natural dulness of fancy and imagination.
Carlyle has described his "bright-beaming, swift
and piercing hazel eyes, with their accompaniment
of rapid keen expression in the other lineaments
of face. He was," he adds, "by no means the
supreme in criticism or anything else; but it is
certain there has no critic appeared among us
since who was worth naming beside him." [2]
Nevertheless, with all his fine endowments, he
could discover in the great poet of Nature little
beyond talent displayed and notoriety courted.

[1] *Edinburgh Review*, November, 1814, p. 4.
[2] Carlyle's "Reminiscences," ed. 1881, ii. 65.

I would be content as a warning to all critics to reprint this review of his with one single note. It should consist of the quotation, without a single word of comment, of the following lines, almost unrivalled, in my belief, in the beauty of the thought and the perfection of the language and the rhythm by any poem of any poet in this century :—

> " Three years she grew in sun and shower,
> Then Nature said, ' A lovelier flower
> On earth was never sown ;
> This Child I to myself will take ;
> She shall be mine, and I will make
> A Lady of my own.
>
> ' Myself will to my darling be
> Both law and impulse : and with me
> The Girl in rock and plain,
> In earth and heaven, in glade and bower,
> Shall feel an overseeing power
> To kindle or restrain
>
> ' She shall be sportive as the Fawn
> That wild with glee across the lawn
> Or up the mountain springs ;
> And hers shall be the breathing balm,
> And hers the silence and the calm
> Of mute insensate things.
>
> ' The floating Clouds their state shall lend
> To her ; for her the willow bend ;
> Nor shall she fail to see

Even in the motions of the Storm
Grace that shall mould the Maiden's form
      By silent sympathy.

' The Stars of midnight shall be dear
To her ; and she shall lean her ear
      In many a secret place
Where Rivulets dance their wayward round,
And beauty born of murmuring sound
      Shall pass into her face.

' And vital feelings of delight
Shall rear her form to stately height,
      Her virgin bosom swell ;
Such thoughts to Lucy I will give
While she and I together live
      Here in this happy Dell.'

Thus Nature spake—The work was done—
How soon my Lucy's race was run !
      She died, and left to me
This heath, this calm and quiet scene ;
The memory of what has been,
      And never more will be."

The critic who could charge Wordsworth with
courting notoriety when he wrote these lines,
might in an earlier age have charged Gray with
courting undertakers when he wrote his " Elegy."
Jeffrey lived long enough to see his judgment-seat
scorned and deserted by a younger generation.
Fourteen years after he declared that Wordsworth
with all his great natural gifts was " finally lost

to the good cause of poetry," a young thinker, who had been trained in the straightest school of the Utilitarians, found in the despised poet that mental relief which in his misery he had elsewhere sought in vain. "I had learnt by experience," writes John Stuart Mill, "that the passive susceptibilities needed to be cultivated as well as the active capacities, and required to be nourished and enriched as well as guided. . . . The cultivation of the feelings became one of the cardinal points in my ethical and philosophical creed. . . . I now began to find meaning in the things which I had read or heard about the importance of poetry and art as instruments of human culture." He goes on to describe the curious dejection into which he had fallen, and the vain attempts which he had made to find relief in books. Byron he had tried, but from him he got no good. He took up Wordsworth, and found in his poems a medicine for his mind in that "they expressed not mere outward beauty, but states of feeling, and of thought coloured by feeling, under the excitement of beauty. "They seemed," he continues, "to be the very culture of the feelings which I was in quest of. . . . I found that he, too, had had similar experience to mine ; that he also had felt that the first freshness of youthful enjoyment of life was not lasting ;

but that he had sought for compensation, and
found it in the way in which he was now teaching
me to find it. The result was that I gradually, but
completely, emerged from my habitual depression,
and was never again subject to it." He met John
Sterling, whose life Carlyle has so admirably
written. "He told me," says Mill, "how he and
others had looked upon me (from hearsay information) as a ' made ' or manufactured man, having
had a certain impress of opinion stamped on me
which I could only reproduce ; and what a change
took place in his feelings when he found that
Wordsworth, and all which that name implies,
' belonged ' to me as much as to him and his
friends." [1]

However strongly the current of opinion set in
a new direction, it swept past the old reviewer,
and left him unmoved and unchanged. Jeffrey, in
his old age, finding how highly Wordsworth was
thought of, "resolved to re-peruse his poems, and
see if he had anything to retract." He was com-
forted by discovering that "except perhaps a con-
temptuous and flippant phrase or two" there was
nothing to withdraw.[2]

There is a fine passage in Thackeray's "New-

[1] " Autobiography of J. S. Mill," pp. 143, 148, 155.
[2] " Diary of H. C. Robinson," iii. 140.

comes " where we read how the old Colonel was
puzzled when he gathered round him at dinner
his son's literary friends, " and the merits of their
poets and writers were discussed with the claret.
. . . He heard opinions that amazed and bewildered
him. He heard that Byron was no great poet,
though a very clever man. He heard that there
had been a wicked persecution against Mr. Pope's
memory and fame, and that it was time to reinstate
him; that his favourite, Dr. Johnson, talked admirably, but did not write English; that young
Keats was a genius to be estimated in future days
with young Raphael; and that a young gentleman of Cambridge, who had lately published two
volumes of verses, might take rank with the
greatest poets of all. Dr. Johnson not write
English! Lord Byron not one of the greatest
poets of the world! Sir Walter a poet of the
second order! Mr. Pope attacked for inferiority
and want of imagination! Mr. Keats and this
young Mr. Tennyson of Cambridge the chief of
modern poetic literature! What were these new
dicta, which Mr. Warrington delivered with a puff
of tobacco smoke; to which Mr. Honeyman
blandly assented, and Clive listened with pleasure?
Such opinions were not of the Colonel's time. He
tried in vain to construe ' Œnone,' and to make

sense of 'Lamia.' 'Ulysses' he could understand;
but what were these prodigious laudations bestowed
on it? And that reverence for Mr. Wordsworth,
what did it mean? Had he not written 'Peter
Bell,' and been turned into deserved ridicule by all
the reviews? Was that dreary 'Excursion' to be
compared to Goldsmith's 'Traveller,' or Dr. Johnson's 'Imitation of the Tenth Satire of Juvenal'?
If the young men told the truth, where had been
the truth in his own young days; and in what
ignorance had our forefathers been brought up?
—Mr. Addison was only an elegant essayist and
shallow trifler! All these opinions were openly
uttered over the Colonel's claret, as he and Mr.
Binnie sat wondering at the speakers who were
knocking the gods of their youth about their
ears." [1]

Our gods, let us raise them on as lofty pedestals
as we please, and fall down before them as low as
we can, let us crown them with wreaths and chap-
lets, and send up the incense before them in clouds,
will, if only we live long enough, in all likelihood
be knocked about our ears too. The more extravagant has been our adoration, the worse will
be the belabouring which they will receive. "Be it
known unto you, oh past generation," our children

[1] "The Newcomes," chap. xxi.

will say, "that we will not serve your gods, nor worship the golden images which you have set up." In their rebellion they may even go a step further, and maintain that the images were not golden, but only gilt.

Mr. Ruskin, writing in the year 1857, when he had all the ripeness of a man not far off his fortieth year, said : "Mrs. Browning's 'Aurora Leigh' is, so far as I know, the greatest poem which the century has produced in any language." Why in the century, among foreigners, Goethe and Victor Hugo, among Englishmen, Wordsworth, Scott, Keats, Shelley, Byron, Landor, Tennyson, and Browning had written either all or at least many of their greatest poems. Before the best that the greatest of these men wrote is to be placed "Aurora Leigh"! Our amazement at such an assertion may be tempered by respect, but, nevertheless, amazement it remains. "Of reflective prose," says the same writer, "read chiefly Bacon, Johnson, and Helps." It is not easy to preserve one's gravity at this strange fellowship. I can picture to myself the feelings, first of bewilderment, and then almost of despair, of some ardent disciple of the great master, as he passed from Bacon's "Essays" through the "Rambler" and "Rasselas" to Sir Arthur Helps's "Friends in Council." I once tried a few pages of

it, but gave it up as hopelessly commonplace. He
has one chance for immortality; he may be remembered as the otherwise unknown author who
was classed by Mr. Ruskin with Bacon and Johnson.[1]

Two hundred years ago there was a City poet,
Elkanah Settle by name, of whom John Wilkes
said: "Elkanah Settle sounds so queer, who can
expect much from that name?" At one time,
nevertheless, he was the rival of the great Dryden.
"Such," says Johnson, "are the revolutions of
fame, or such is the prevalence of fashion, that
the man whose works have not yet been thought
to deserve the care of collecting them, who died
forgotten in an hospital, and whose latter years
were spent in contriving shows for fairs, and carrying an elegy or epithalamium, of which the beginning and end were occasionally varied, but the in-
termediate parts were always the same, to every
house where there was a funeral or a wedding,
might with truth have had inscribed upon his
stone:

"'Here lies the rival and antagonist of Dryden.'"[2]

Violent indeed are the revolutions in taste which

---

[1] "Elements of Drawing," 1st ed., p. 348.
[2] Johnson's "Works," ed. 1825, vii. 277.

the world has seen. Southey, writing fifty years
ago about those books of which the copyright was
of the greatest value, says that within his recol-
lection among the five most valuable of all would
have been Blair's "Lectures on Rhetoric" and
Blair's "Sermons."[1]   In Mr. Alfred Morrison's
great collection of autographs is a letter from
Blair's publisher, William Strahan, announcing a
draft of £500 as the last payment for the "Lectures
on Rhetoric." What the previous payments had
been I do not know. How popular his sermons
once were the bookstalls still testify ; into what
neglect they have fallen is shown by the price at
which they are offered for sale. Three-quarters of
a century after the death of the poet John Pomfret
it was said, that "perhaps no composition in our
language had been oftener perused than his
"Choice."[2]   Another quarter of a century passed,
and the hundred years were complete ; yet we
find Southey asking : " Why is Pomfret the most
popular of the English poets ? The fact is certain,
and the solution would be useful."[3]   It is not un-
likely that there is no one in this room but myself
who has read this poem. Let me read therefore

---

[1] Southey's " Life and Letters," vi. 355.
[2] Johnson's " Works," vii. 222.
[3] Southey's " Specimens," i. 91.

to you a few lines, that you may judge of the value
of popularity as a test :

> " If Heaven the grateful liberty would give,
> That I might choose my method how to live,
> And all those hours, propitious Fate should lend
> In blissful ease and satisfaction spend ;
> Near some fair town I'd have a private seat,
> Built uniform ; not little, not too great ;
> Better, if on a rising ground it stood,
> On this side fields, on that a neighb'ring wood ;
> It should within no other things contain
> But what are useful, necessary, plain :
> Methinks 'tis nauseous, and I'd ne'er endure
> The needless pomp of gaudy furniture.
> A little garden, grateful to the eye,
> And a cool rivulet run murm'ring by,
> On whose delicious banks a stately row
> Of shady limes or sycamores should grow ;
> At th' end of which a silent study plac'd
> Should be with all the noblest authors grac'd."

Our grandfathers or our great - grandfathers
might with some fair show of reason have
maintained that it was impossible to believe that
a poem which had so well stood the test of time
would ever sink into forgetfulness. Let me
suggest to you that if any one in your hearing
foretells immortality for some writer for whom
you have no relish, you should ask him at once
whether he has read Pomfret's " Choice."

I will contrast with these lines that fine

passage in which Johnson also describes a choice of life. He tells the story of his own early years; he recounts the eager hopes with which he had entered this great university, and the ills which had assailed him in the outside world. In his old age, when he was prosperous and famous, he one day read the lines aloud. As all the troubles he had undergone trooped back to his memory he burst into a passion of tears. So in the court of Alcinous Ulysses wept when he heard the sweet singer tell of the sufferings of the Achæans beneath the walls of Troy.

"When first the college rolls receive his name,
The young enthusiast quits his ease for fame;
Through all his veins the fever of renown
Spreads from the strong contagion of the gown;
O'er Bodley's dome his future labours spread,
And Bacon's mansion trembles o'er his head.
Are these thy views? Proceed, illustrious youth,
And virtue guard thee to the throne of truth!
Yet, should thy soul indulge the gen'rous heat
Till captive science yields her last retreat;
Should reason guide thee with her brightest ray,
And pour on misty doubt resistless day;
Should no false kindness lure to loose delight,
Nor praise relax, nor difficulty fright;
Should tempting novelty thy cell refrain,
And sloth effuse her opiate fumes in vain;
Should beauty blunt on fops her fatal dart,
Nor claim the triumph of a letter'd heart;
Should no disease thy torpid veins invade,

Nor melancholy's phantoms haunt thy shade ;
Yet hope not life from grief or danger free,
Nor think the doom of man revers'd for thee :
Deign on the passing world to turn thine eyes,
And pause awhile from letters, to be wise ;
There mark what ills the scholar's life assail,
Toil, envy, want, the patron, and the gaol.
See nations, slowly wise and meanly just,
To buried merit raise the tardy bust.
If dreams yet flatter, once again attend,
Hear Lydiat's life, and Galileo's end."

The last line of manuscript that Sir Walter
Scott sent to press, the line with which he closed
his glorious series of poems and romances, was a
quotation from the "Vanity of Human Wishes."

If popularity is the measure of merit the payment of the publisher is often the measure of
popularity.   Tried by this standard how ridiculous
is the general judgment.   Goldsmith, when asked
at a Royal Academy dinner whether he was going
to bring out a new poem, replied: "I cannot
afford to court the draggle-tail muses, they would
let me starve."   He had already given to the
world his "Traveller" and "Deserted Village."
He had not been dead twenty years when
Erasmus Darwin, for the second part of his
"Botanic Garden," was paid a thousand guineas
—just fifty times as much as Goldsmith had
received for "The Traveller," sixty-six times as

much as Johnson had received for the second of his great poems, "The Vanity of Human Wishes," and more than a hundred times as much as Milton had received for the "Paradise Lost." Wordsworth's "Lyrical Ballads," and Coleridge's "Ancient Mariner," which were published together in one small volume fell still-born from the press. Five hundred copies were printed, but so few were sold that the publisher parted with the bulk of them to a bookseller at a loss. The copyright was looked upon as worthless, and was returned to the authors. Wordsworth had almost reached the age of fifty when in a letter to a friend, he said : " I have never been much of a salesman in matters of literature ; the whole of my returns —I do not say my *net-profits*, but *returns* from the writing trade not amounting to seven-score pounds."[1] By this time he had written all his finest poems — almost all that are included in Matthew Arnold's selection—and the wages of these long years did not amount to the sum that a leading barrister or a fashionable physician sometimes makes in a single day. He had need of plain living to support his high thinking.

Robertson, for his second work, " The History of Charles V.," was paid £3,800, while Thomas

[1] Wordsworth's "Life," ed. 1851, i. 122 ; ii. 207.

Carlyle, after twenty years of such labour as
Robertson never dreamed of, had not been able
with all his copyrights and his current earnings to
stretch his average yearly income beyond £150.
If his " French Revolution" failed, as his other
books had failed, " he had resolved to abandon
literature, buy spade and rifle, and make for the
backwoods of America." [1] He had reached his
fortieth year when he was thus hovering almost
on the brink of despair.

According to Addison " men of the best sense
are always diffident of their private judgment till
it receives a sanction from the public. *Provoco ad
populum*," he continues, " I appeal to the people,
was the usual saying of a very excellent dramatic
poet, when he had any disputes with particular
persons about the justness and regularity of his
productions." [2] In many cases, however, the
appeal to the people was worse even than the
appeal to the Court of Chancery in the days of
old.   Unless the suitor in these literary cases had
means of his own he was likely to die of hunger
long before the final decision in his favour was
given.   "What porridge had John Keats?"   Even
when the decision has been given how wavering

[1] Froude's " Life of Carlyle," Part I. ii. 477 ; Part II. ii. 161.
[2] *The Guardian*, No. 98.

often is the execution of the sentence! If I can trust my judgment no nobler chapter in biography has been published these latter years than Carlyle's brief life of his father, the stonemason of Ecclefechan. It was written nearly sixty years ago, when his style was at its best ; written, too, under deep feeling, for it was composed in "the first dark days of death." It is a noble picture of honest work and honest poverty, and manly independence. It is a sermon on the text, "We dare be poor for all that," and the preacher is not unworthy of the poet. It is the very gospel of labour. I would have it a reading book in every school in England—in Eton and Harrow, that they might learn there the unworthiness of idleness ; in Whitechapel and Stoke Pogis, that they might learn there the full dignity of labour. There would soon be no hanging the head for honest poverty. I know how it has encouraged me. As day after day, week after week, and month after month I once toiled at a long, and heavy, and dull piece of work, where the greatest accuracy was needed, I was cheered and strengthened by the thought of the old Scottish stonemason so doing his work that it should never have to be done again. "Let me write my books as he built his houses," was his son's prayer,

This admirable memoir was published with Carlyle's other "Reminiscences" as they are called. In the rest of the book there was not a little that justly roused indignation, and even anger, so harsh, so arrogant, I might even say so insolent was often his judgment of his contemporaries. Nevertheless, with all its faults it is irradiated by genius. With a rapid touch, but with the touch of a master, we have sketched for us the likenesses of many a man and woman renowned in the literary world of London. We have the author's own likeness drawn by himself with innumerable strokes—a man well worth studying, for he was cast in no common mould. We must go back to Samuel Johnson before we can find his fellow in the strangeness and the rugged strength of his character. The book came, as it were, like a gift from the grave of one who, if never popular, was at all events famous. Editor and publisher alike must, with good reason, have counted on a great sale. It reached no second edition. Some years later, it is true, by a rival editor a revised text was brought out, but this was due, not to the popular demand, but to the natural and proper desire to correct the strange blunders of the editor, transcriber, or printer. Yet this is the age of reminiscences and memoirs. Men who do not know how to write recount what was never worth the telling. They publish what they call their recollections. Their foolish and impertinent gossip is eagerly brought up. It satisfies, to borrow Coleridge's words, "those two contrary yet co-existing propensities of human nature, indulgence of sloth and hatred of vacancy." " This genus of amusement," he continues, " comprises as its species, gaming, swinging or swaying on a chair or gate, spitting over a bridge, smoking, snuff-taking, *tête-à-tête* quarrels after dinner between husband and wife; conning word by word all the advertisements of the *Daily Advertiser* in a public house on a rainy day," &c., &c., &c.[1] These memoirs have their day just as their authors have their money.

> " The earth hath bubbles, as the water has,
> And these are of them."

One hundred years hence Carlyle's rugged character will still interest the world and his "Reminiscences" will still be read. Perhaps some editor, a harmless drudge, will almost swamp the text beneath an inundation of footnotes.

The judgments of men of letters and even of genius are scarcely less faulty than those of the

[1] Coleridge's " Biographia Literaria," p. 24.

common run. I once had in my study an un-published autograph letter of David Hume, dated January 30, 1773. It is written to his friend and publisher, William Strahan, who had done all that a friend and publisher could do to induce him to carry his "History" two or three reigns beyond the Revolution. Even George III. had interested himself in this, and in augmenting the historian's pension had laid it down as a condition that he should continue his "History." Not a single chapter for all that did he add.[1] When Strahan found that his friend was obstinate in the indolence of £1,100 a year, he suggested that the task should be put into the hands of some other writer.

Hume replied :

"Considering the Treatment I have met with, it would have been very silly for me at my years to continue writing any more; and still more blameless to warp my Principles and Sentiments in conformity to the Prejudices of a stupid, factious Nation, with whom I am heartily disgusted.

[1] Smollett's continuation is, properly speaking, no continuation at all; it is merely the concluding part of that writer's "Complete History of England, from the descent of Julius Cæsar to the Treaty of Aix-la-Chapelle in 1748," which was published earlier than six of the eight octavo volumes of which Hume's "History" is composed.

"I wish my Continuators good Success; though I believe they have sense enough not to care whether they meet with it or not. Macpherson has Style and Spirit, but is hot-headed, and consequently without Judgment. Sir John Dalrymple has Spirit, but no Style, and still less Judgment than the other. I should think Dr. Douglas, if he would undertake it, a better hand than either. Or what think you of Andrew Stuart? For as to any Englishman, that Nation is so sunk in Stupidity and Barbarism and Faction that you may as well think of Lapland for an author. The best Book that has been writ by any Englishman these thirty years (for Dr. Franklyn is an American) is 'Tristram Shandy,' bad as it is; a Remark which may astonish you, but which you will find true on Reflection." [1]

You may well wonder how Dr. Franklin's name got hitched in here. It is highly probable that Hume, who was a thorough Frenchman in his love of paying pretty compliments, thought that this passage would be shown to the American philosopher. Strahan had added as a postscript to his last letter, which Hume had just received: "Dr. Franklin, who sits at my elbow, desires

[1] "Letters of David Hume to William Strahan," ed. by G. B. Hill, p. 255.

to be affectionately remembered to you, and to
your worthy sister, who was so kind to him." In
whatever way it came to pass that he was mentioned, Hume clearly implies that his books were
better than any that had been written by Englishmen within the last thirty years. That period had
not, it is true, been so rich in great works as many
other periods in our history. Nevertheless, even
when the works of Irishmen, Scotchmen, and
Welshmen were excluded, it could boast of having
given birth to " Clarissa " and " Sir Charles
Grandison," " Tom Jones " and " Amelia," the
great Dictionary, the " Rambler " and " Rasselas,"
Blackstone's "Commentaries," Collins' "Odes," and
all Gray's " Poems." In "this nation so sunk in
stupidity and barbarism and faction," this Lapland
. . . " This blessed plot, this earth, this realm, this
England "—it had once been called—in it, I say,
at the time when this peevish genius was writing
were living, of various ages, some with their life
well-nigh lived, others with it just begun, but all
born of English stock—Samuel Johnson, with his
" Lives of the Poets " not yet written ; Horace
Walpole, with his " Letters " not yet published ;
Gibbon, with his "History of the Decline and Fall "
already begun ; Blackstone, Cowper, Jeremy Bentham, Fanny Burney, Crabbe, Porson, Cobbett,

Wordsworth, Coleridge, and Sydney Smith. No
bad show for Lapland! Wordsworth, we might
almost suspect, had felt the reproach that was thus
cast upon his cradle, for, speaking of Adam Smith,
he called him, "the worst critic, David Hume not
excepted, that Scotland, a soil to which this sort
of weed seems natural, has produced." [1]

A prophecy which Hume made about Rousseau
is not less absurd than the judgment which he
passed on English men of letters. At first there
were few who thought more highly than he did of
that unhappy genius. " I revere his greatness of
mind," he wrote, " which makes him fly obligations
and dependence, and I have the vanity to think
that through the course of my life I have en-
deavoured to resemble him in those maxims." He
places him "among the first writers of the age."
His "Treatise on Education" "carries," he says,
"the stamp of a great genius ; and what enhances
its beauty, the stamp of a very particular genius."
Suddenly Rousseau, in one of his fits of wild suspicion, in a letter that bears the mark both of
genius and madness, attacked his friend and bene-
factor. "He has had," wrote Hume to Adam
Smith, "the satisfaction during a time of being
much talked of; the thing in the world he most

[1] Wordsworth's " Works," ed. 1857, vi. 367.

desires; but it has been at the expense of being consigned to perpetual neglect and oblivion." [1] Into what kind of neglect and oblivion Rousseau was to fall was shown two-and-twenty years after this letter was written, by the outbreak of the French Revolution.

It was not, however, only Scotchmen among men of letters who last century were absurd in their judgments. Goldsmith says of Dante that "he addressed a barbarous people in a method suited to their apprehensions; united Purgatory and the River Styx, St. Peter and Virgil, heaven and hell together, and shows a strange mixture of good sense and absurdity. The truth is he owes most of his reputation to the obscurity of the times in which he lived." [2] When Horace Walpole saw Garrick for the first time he wrote: "All the run is now after Garrick, a wine merchant, who is turned player at Goodman's Fields. He plays all parts, and is a very good mimic. His acting I have seen, and may say to you, who will not tell it again here, I see nothing wonderful in it." [3] Gray agreed with Walpole in this. "Did I tell you

[1] "Letters of David Hume to William Strahan," pp. 78, 83.

[2] "An Enquiry into the Present State of Polite Learning," chap. iv.

[3] Walpole's "Letters," i. 168.

about Mr. Garrick," he writes, "that the town are
horn-mad after? There are a dozen dukes of a
night at Goodman's Fields sometimes ; and yet
I am stiff in the opposition." [1] Only nine years
after the last volume of Sterne's great novel was
published—a work which I venture to think is as
likely to be immortal as it is certainly immoral—
Johnson said : " Nothing odd will do long. ' Tristram Shandy ' did not last." Horace Walpole
called it " the dregs of nonsense." Goldsmith
described Sterne as a blockhead, and worse than a
blockhead. Dr. Farmer, Master of Emmanuel College, Cambridge, the eminent Shakesperian critic,
said one day to the younger members of that
society : " You young men seem very fond of this
' Tristram Shandy ' ; but mark my words, however
much it may be talked about at present, yet,
depend upon it, in the course cf twenty years
should any one wish to refer to it he will be
obliged to go to an antiquary to inquire for
it." [2] The young men grew, we may hope, to be
old men, but the learned critic's words they never
saw come true. Six-and-thirty years after Sterne's
first volume had been published Thomas Car-

---

[1] Gray's " Works," ed. 1858, ii. 185.
[2] Boswell's " Life of Johnson," ed. by G. B. Hill, ii. **173,**
449.

lyle was born. He was as bad as the undergraduates of the Cambridge College. " My
first favourite books," he writes, " had been
' Hudibras ' and ' Tristram Shandy.' " Sterne he
describes " as our last specimen of humour,
and with all his faults our best; our finest
if not our strongest ; for Yorick and Corporal
Trim and Uncle Toby have yet no brother but
in Don Quixote, far as he lies above them."
Macaulay was no better than Carlyle. He cele-
brates "the exquisite skill with which Sterne
delineates a veteran who had fought at the
Boyne and at Namur."[1] If Dr. Farmer could see
nothing in " Tristram Shandy," a far greater man
could see nothing in Voltaire's " Candide." " I
could not read it for the dulness," wrote Charles
Lamb.[2]

Hume wrote of John Home's play of " Douglas,"
which lives, so far as it does live, somewhat
ridiculously in the line, " My name is Norval."
Hume, I say, wrote of this play : " I am persuaded
it will be esteemed the best, and by French critics,
the only tragedy of our language." He would

[1] Froude's " Life of Carlyle," part i., vol. i. p. 396 ; Carlyle's " Miscellaneous Essays," i. 13; Macaulay's " History
of England," ed. 1873, iii. 169.
[2] Lamb's " Letters," ed. by A. Ainger, i. 277.

have joined in the cry of the gods of the gallery of the Edinburgh theatre, "Where's Wully Shakespeare noo?" Dedicating to the author an edition of his Essays, he says: "You possess the true theatric genius of Shakespeare and Otway, refined from the unhappy barbarism of the one, and licentiousness of the other?" In the Appendix to the reign of James I. in his "History of England," he writes of Shakespeare: "His total ignorance of all theatrical art and conduct, however material a defect, yet as it affects the spectator rather than the reader, we can more easily excuse, than that want of taste which often prevails in his productions, and which gives way only by intervals to the irradiations of genius."[1]

Adam Smith was not inferior to his friend in perversity of taste. He regretted that in comedy the English writers had not followed the model of the French school in the use of rhyme. It is to him more than to any other man that we owe freedom of commerce. It was he who struck off the fetters which cramped industry and trade. But great as is our debt to him, we can hardly forgive him for the wish that Shakespeare's humour had been taught to pace in trammels, and

[1] See notes in my edition, "Letters of David Hume to William Strahan," pp. 11–16.

that honest Jack Falstaff and Dogberry had never opened their mouths except in rhyming couplets. Racine's "Phædra" he looked upon as "perhaps the finest tragedy that is extant in any language."[1] Let me not forget, however, to do justice to the great economist. In the list of subscribers to the second edition of Burns's poems his name is entered for four copies.

Even Burns himself does not fall short of his famous countrymen in absurdity. In one of his prologues, speaking of Scotland, he says :

"Here Douglas forms wild Shakespeare into plan."

As we read these extravagant laudations of this new dramatist we are pleased at recalling that there was one great writer who was not cheated into mistaking "this farthing candle for the northern lights." It was in a coffee-house in this very city of Oxford that "Dr. Johnson called to old Mr. Sheridan, 'How came you, sir, to give Home a gold medal for writing that foolish play?' and defied him to show ten good lines in it." Sir Walter Scott, writing little more than sixty years ago, maintained that "Douglas was a masterpiece." He added : "Even that does not stand

[1] Stewart's "Life of Adam Smith," p. 71, and Smith's "Theory of Moral Sentiments," ed. 1801, i. 255.

the closet. Its merits are for the stage; and it is certainly one of the best acting plays going." [1] It must be many a day since it has been represented, at all events on the London stage.

Garrick, it might be thought, would have had truer taste as regards Shakespeare, "the god of his idolatry," than many of his contemporaries. Yet he exulted that he lived long enough to rescue Hamlet " from all the rubbish of the fifth act." " I have," he wrote, a few months before his retirement, " brought 'Hamlet' forth without the gravedigger's trick and the fencing match." [2]

[1] Boswell's " Life of Johnson," ii. 320 ; v. 360.
[2] " Garrick Correspondence," ii. 126.

LECTURE II.

LECTURE II.

IF we turn to an earlier century, we can see, in the rise of what is called Pindarism, how even men of great genius whose youthful breeding was not in the artificiality of the age of Queen Anne, and of the first two Georges, but in one of the noblest ages of literature, could, nevertheless, be depraved in taste. Cowley, who was born but two years after Shakespeare's death, while those mighty masters of prose, the translators of the great English Bible were many of them still living, looking upon the Pindaric Odes as one of the lost inventions of antiquity, "made a bold and vigorous attempt to recover them." There can be no question that for many a long year Cowley had far more readers than Shakespeare or Milton. He was the founder of a new style of composition which prevailed about half a century, and even then was slow in dying out. " Clarendon represents him as having taken a flight beyond all that went before him ; and Milton is said to have declared that the three greatest English poets were Spenser, Shakespeare, and Cowley." [1]   He was the darling of Dryden's youth. Addison, in his lines on " The Greatest English Poets," after justly censuring him as

> " O'er-run with wit, and lavish of his thought ; "

who

> " More had pleased us, had he pleased us less,"

goes on to say :

> " Pardon, great poet, that I dare to name
> The unnumbered beauties of thy verse with blame."

In twenty-five years, between 1656 and 1681, seven folio editions of his works were published. The first edition of Shakespeare had been brought out thirty-three years before Cowley's first; but his fourth not till four years after Cowley's seventh. The " Paradise Lost," though it seems among readers to have been superior in popularity to Shakespeare, was inferior to Cowley, for of it in twenty-one years only four editions were required.

[1] Johnson's " Works," ed. 1825, vii. 36, 49.

Milton was less applauded even than Waller.
Well does Dr. Warton write : " The noble confidence and strength of mind in Milton is not in
any circumstance more visible and more admirable
than his writing a poem in a style and manner
that he was sure would not be relished or regarded
by his corrupt contemporaries." [1]

> " Though fallen on evil days,
> On evil days though fallen and evil tongues,"

he yet could say :

> " Still govern thou my song,
> Urania, and fit audience find, though few."

Cowley's popularity gradually waned. He had
been dead about fourscore years when Pope
asked :

> " Who now reads Cowley ? "

while a few years later we find Samuel Richardson,
the novelist, wondering that he was so absolutely
neglected.[2] We may smile at the false taste which
placed Cowley before Milton and both Cowley and
Milton before Shakespeare. Yet had we been
living then, unless we had been blest with a singu-

---

[1] Warton's " Pope's Works," vol. i. pp. lv. 286.
[2] Pope's " Imitations of Horace," epis. ii. i. 75, and
Richardson's " Correspondence," ii. 229.

larly piercing judgment, we should in all likelihood
have been as confident in our admiration of the
favourite of our age as the members of the
Browning Club can be in their worship of Mr.
Browning. Let me read to you one of Cowley's
Pindaric Odes to show you what was the style at
which this great poet aimed in the conviction, as
he avowed, that " it was the highest and noblest
kind of writing in verse." [1]

THE PRAISE OF PINDAR.

I.

Pindar is imitable by none ;
The Phœnix Pindar is a vast species alone.
Who e're but Dædalus with waxen wings could **fly**
And neither sink too low, nor soar too high ?
    What could he who follow'd claim,
But of vain boldness the unhappy fame,
    And by his fall a Sea to name ?
    Pindars unnavigable Song
Like a swoln Flood from some steep Mountain pours along.
    The Ocean meets with such a Voice
From his enlarged Mouth, as drowns the Oceans noise.

II.

So Pindar does new Words and Figures roul
Down his impetuous Dithyrambique Tyde,
    Which in no Channel deigns t' abide,
    Which neither Banks nor Dikes controul.
    Whether th' Immortal Gods he sings
    In a no less Immortal strain,

---

[1] Johnson's "Works," vii. 41.

Or the great Acts of God-descended Kings,
Who in his Numbers still survive and Reign.
 Each rich embroidered Line,
Which their triumphant Brows around,
 By his sacred Hand is bound,
Does all their starry Diadems outshine.

III.

Whether at Pisa's race he please
To carve in polisht Verse the Conqu'erors Images,
Whether the Swift, the Skilful, or the Strong,
Be crowned in his Nimble, Artful, Vigorous Song :
Whether some brave young mans untimely fate
In words worth Dying for he celebrate,
 Such mournful, and such pleasing words,
As joy to his Mothers and his Mistress grief affords :
 He bids him live and Grow in fame,
 Among the Stars he sticks his Name :
The Grave can but the Dross of him devour,
So small is Deaths, so great the Poets power.

IV.

Lo, how th' obsequious Wind, and swelling Air
 The Theban Swan does upwards bear
Into the walks of Clouds, where he does play,
And with extended Wings opens his liquid way.
 Whilst alas, my tim'erous Muse
 Unambitious tracks pursues ;
 Does with weak unballast wings,
 About the Mossy Brooks and Springs,
 About the Trees new-blossom'd Heads,
 About the Gardens painted Beds,
 About the Fields and flowry Meads,
 And all inferiour beauteous things
 Like the laborious Bee,
 For little drops of Honey flee,
And there with Humble Sweets contents her Industrie.

Strained and unnatural though this Ode is, nevertheless it has great vigour of thought and some beautiful lines. It contains one noble couplet, or at least one noble half line :—

> "Whether some brave young man's untimely fate
> In words worth dying for he celebrate."

If Cowley's thoughts are "most fantastic and out of the way," they are nevertheless expressed "in the most pure and genuine mother English." [1]

How it came to pass that "Pindarism," our "Pindaric infatuation," "our Pindaric madness," "the Pindaric folly," as Johnson justly styled it, became so popular that great critic has clearly pointed out. "This lax and lawless versification," he says, "so much concealed the deficiencies of the barren and flattered the laziness of the idle, that it immediately overspread our books of poetry; all the boys and girls caught the pleasing fashion, and they that could do nothing else could write like Pindar." [2] This sentence with the change of one or two words is applicable to every age. It is not only laxness and lawlessness that are caught; smoothness and regularity have their day too. All the boys and girls of every generation catch the

[1] Coleridge's "Biographia Literaria," p. 11.
[2] Johnson's "Works," vii. 41.

pleasing fashion, and they who can do nothing else can write like Pindar, or Pope, or Johnson, or Byron, or Carlyle, or Macaulay, or Browning, or the modern art critics, or the female novelists, or the gentlemen whose easy task it is to fill a column and a third of the newspaper with what is called descriptive writing. What we can do easily and successfully that we admire and uphold ; our self-interest gets hopelessly entangled with our judgment, and we set up as critics and prophets when we are at best self-deceived advocates. Even if we do not write we get scarcely less interested in the cause as readers. It is our taste, we feel that is on its trial quite as much as the taste of the writer whom we have set up as an idol. " What ? " asks Pope, " must be the priest, where a monkey is the god ? " What, we ask, must be our state, if our great writer can be shown to be a mere pretentious piece of wordiness ? It is no doubt true, as Coleridge has pointed out, in his curious history of his own mental growth, that " no models of past times, however perfect, can have the same vivid effect on the youthful mind as the productions of contemporary genius. . . . The great works of past ages," he continues, " seem to a young man things of another race, in respect to which his faculties must remain passive and submiss, even

as to the stars and mountains. But the writings
of a contemporary, perhaps not many years older
than himself, surrounded by the same circumstances and disciplined by the same manners,
possess a reality for him, and inspire an actual
friendship as of a man for a man. His very admiration is the wind which fans and feeds his hope.
The poems themselves assume the properties of
flesh and blood. To recite, to extol, to contend
for them is but the payment of a debt due to one
who exists to receive it."

The wind which fanned and fed Coleridge's hope
and the hope of Southey and Wordsworth, too,
was their admiration of a poet but a few years
their senior, William Lisle Bowles. His life was
prolonged to a great age. He outlived two of his
three disciples and his own fame. The gentle old
man was in no illusion about himself. "Many
years," he wrote, "after my gray head shall have
been laid at rest, some of those who may have seen
those poems of which Coleridge spoke in the days
of his earliest song so enthusiastically may inquire,
'Who was W. L. Bowles?'"[1] It was this minor
poet, then, who gave the first impulse to two men of
great genius; but had they read Bowles alone, or the

[1] Coleridge's "Biographia Literaria," p. 5; Knight's
"Cyclopædia of Biography," i. 875.

school of Bowles, neither Coleridge nor Wordsworth would sit where they now sit on the serene heights. It was by the great poets of all ages that their thoughts had been nourished and their minds disciplined. Coleridge speaks with gratitude of "the very sensible, though very severe" Master of Christ's Hospital, by whom his youthful taste had been formed. "He early moulded it to the preference of Demosthenes to Cicero, of Homer and Theocritus to Virgil, and again of Virgil to Ovid. . . . He made us read Shakespeare and Milton as lessons. . . . In the truly great poets, he would say, there is a reason assignable not only for every word, but for the position of every word. In our own English compositions he showed no mercy to phrase, metaphor, or image unsupported by a sound sense, or where the same sense might have been conveyed with equal force and dignity in plainer words. Lute, harp, lyre, muse, muses and inspirations, Pegasus, Parnassus, and Hippocrene were all an abomination to him. I fancy I can almost hear him now exclaiming, 'Harp? Harp? Lyre? Pen and ink, boy, you mean. Muse, boy, muse? Your nurse's daughter you mean. Pierian spring? Oh, aye! the cloister-pump, I suppose.'"[1] To a mind thus disciplined the excessive worship of

[1] "Biographia Literaria," p. 3.

contemporary writers could do little harm, for it was certain not to last long. In Wordsworth it did, I suspect, more mischief. His school training had been less severe. Had he studied more thoroughly the merits of a school of poets whom he disliked, he might have avoided some of those faults of feebleness and tediousness which rouse the contempt of his enemies and the anger of those who love him.

But to return to the more immediate subject of my lectures—the judgments passed on books by the different generations. Bacon was born three years before Shakespeare, and outlived him by ten. A great part of their lives they dwelt in the same town ; they must have jostled each other in the street. Yet the philosopher, it has been pointed out, " in his multifarious writings nowhere either quotes Shakespeare or alludes to him."[1] He is almost worse than the worthy citizen who had lived in Paris during the whole of the Reign of Terror without discovering that anything unusual had been going on. If there were any mind which was capable of at once discovering Shakespeare's transcendent greatness, surely it should have been his who is only second to him among our poets, and who was not separated from him by any gulf

[1] Wordsworth's " Works," vi. 363.

of time. Milton was a boy of seven when Shakespeare died ; he entered Cambridge only about a year after the first folio edition of the collected plays was published. Yet his judgment seems to be little sounder than David Hume's when, in the preface to his " Samson Agonistes," he speaks of Æschylus, Sophocles, and Euripides as " the three tragic poets, unequalled yet by any, and the best rule to all who endeavour to write tragedy," and when he " vindicates tragedy from the small esteem, or rather infamy, which, in the account of many, it undergoes at this day with other common interludes ; happening through the poet's error of intermixing comic stuff with tragic sadness and gravity, or introducing trivial and vulgar persons, which by all judicious hath been counted absurd, and brought in without discretion, corruptly to gratify the people."

This " comic stuff " was, I suppose, much the same as that which Garrick calls " the rubbish of the fifth act of ' Hamlet ; ' " the buffoonery with which Voltaire reproached Shakespeare ; those admirable scenes in which the genius of the mighty poet interwove in the web of life the bright colours with the sad, and showed us man, not as the unities would have him, but as Nature has made him.

Dryden, I must admit, recognised to the full that genius which Milton had seen only in part. In his "Essay of Dramatick Poesie," written in the year 1668, three years earlier than "Samson Agonistes," he had said: "Shakespeare was the man who of all modern, and perhaps ancient, poets, had the largest and most comprehensive soul. All the images of nature were still present to him, and he drew them, not laboriously, but luckily: when he describes anything, you more than see it, you feel it too. Those who accuse him to have wanted learning give him the greater commendation; he was naturally learned; he needed not the spectacles of books to read nature; he looked inwards and found her there. I cannot say he is everywhere alike; were he so, I should do him injury to compare him with the greatest of mankind. He is many times flat, insipid; his comic wit degenerating into clenches,[1] his serious swelling into bombast. But he is always great when some great occasion is presented to him. No man can say he ever had a fit subject for his wit, and did not then raise himself as high above the rest of poets.

[1] "*Clinch*: a pun ; an ambiguity" (Johnson's Dictionary).

' Quantum lenta solent inter viburna cupressi.' " [1]

In his lines to Sir Godfrey Kneller, who, it is conjectured, had sent him a copy of the Chandos portrait of Shakespeare, Dryden says :

> ' Shakespeare, thy gift, I place before my sight,
> With awe I ask his blessing ere I write,
> With reverence look on his majestic face ;
> Proud to be less, but of his god-like race."

But even Dryden, with all his admiration for Shakespeare, ventured to lay an impious hand on " The Tempest," and to re-write it for the stage. He must have known how shameful was his usage ; yet we may perhaps forgive him for one fine passage. He makes Prospero say :

> " On what strange grounds we build our hopes and fears :
> Man's life is all a mist, and in the dark
> Our fortunes meet us."

In spite of the weight which, by his preface, he threw into the scale, the balance swung against Shakespeare till time and the world's long thinking set it right. In Dryden's time, he tells us, two of the plays of Beaumont and Fletcher were acted for one of Shakespeare's. In the two theatres of the Restoration only three of his plays were revived in the one, and about five in the other. For nearly

[1] " As towers the cypress tall above the lowly shrubs."

eighty years "Romeo and Juliet" had lain
neglected by the actors, when Garrick brought it
out at the end of 1748. On March 1, 1662, Pepys
had gone in a coach with his wife to see it, and
had recorded in his diary : " It is a play of itself
the worst that ever I heard, and the worst acted
that ever I saw these people do." [1] But even
Garrick, as I have shown, was little sensible of
the vast genius of Shakespeare, and as he had
" cleared ' Hamlet ' from rubbish," so now he
cobbled that beautiful tragedy, " The Story of
Juliet and her Romeo." He saw, as we are told
by the critic and play-writer, Arthur Murphy, that
the catastrophe might be made more affecting.
He therefore altered the fifth act " and rendered
the catastrophe (I again quote Murphy) the
most affecting in the whole compass of the
drama." [2]

It is an undoubted fact, nevertheless, that Garrick
did much to render Shakespeare more widely
known. In the twenty years before he undertook
the management of Drury Lane "not more than
eight or nine of Shakespeare's comedies and trage-

[1] " An Essay of Dramatick Poesie ; " Dryden's " Plays,"
ed. 1701, i. 20 ; Davies's " Dramatic Miscellanies," iii. 161 ;
Davies's " Life of Garrick," i. 124 ; Pepys's " Diary," ed.
1851, i. 330.
[2] Murphy's " Life of Garrick," p. 100.

dies were in possession of the stage ; " while he used
to have played every year seventeen or eighteen at
his theatre.[1] I find that in five weeks of the
autumn of 1754 there were at the two theatres of
Drury Lane and Covent Garden nineteen nights
on which Shakespeare was acted, and that nine
of his plays were represented—"Hamlet," "Macbeth," "Othello," "Romeo and Juliet," "Corio-
lanus," "Richard III.," "Henry VIII.," "The
Merchant of Venice," and "Much Ado About
Nothing." We have the impudence to despise
the eighteenth century for its ignorance and
neglect of real poetry. London at that time had
but two theatres. In the sixty representations
which were given in these five weeks nineteen were
of plays of Shakespeare. Nor was there anything
unusual in this. Two years earlier in fifty-seven
nights his plays were acted twenty times.[1] The
evil days had not been yet invented of splendid
and costly scenery with long runs, which alone
could pay for the extravagance of the outlay.

It was not only or even chiefly to Garrick that
was due this Shakespearian revival. The great actor
was following the tide, and not heading it. The
ladies, be it said to their honour, some time before

[1] Davies's " Life of Garrick," i. 120.
[2] *Gentleman's Magazine*, 1752, p. 479 ; 1754, p. 532.

his first appearance on the stage, had formed themselves into a Shakespeare Club, and bespoke every
week some favourite play of our immortal poet.[1]
Edition after edition of his works had appeared.
Rowe had been followed by Pope, and Pope by
Theobald, to be soon followed in turn by Hanmer,
Warburton, and Johnson. The eighteenth century
had been satisfied with four editions of his collected
plays. In the first hundred years after his death
there were but six; in the next fifty there were
three-and-twenty.

The reaction from the evil days of the Restoration had long set in. Even Colley Cibber, who
was old enough to have borne arms on the side of
the Prince of Orange in the glorious Revolution,
writing of our great poet, says: "A hundred
years are wasted, and another silent century
well advanced; and yet what unborn age shall
say Shakespeare has his equal?" The Earl
of Shaftesbury, in the reign of Anne—that
age which is reproached for its artificiality—
describes "Hamlet" as the play "which appears
to have most affected English hearts."[2] Nevertheless, in the very year in which this was written

---

[1] Davies's "Life of Garrick," p. 20.
[2] Cibber's "Autobiography," ed. 1826, p. 58; "Characteristics," ed. 1714, i. 275.

a curious instance is to be found of the un-
familiarity of the polite reader with Shakespeare's
less important works. In the *Tatler* for September 30, 1710, a story is told in illustration of
" the proverbial expression of *taking a woman
down in her wedding shoes,* if you would bring her
to reason. An early behaviour of this sort," continues the writer, " had a very remarkable good
effect in a family wherein I was several years an
intimate acquaintance." He goes on to tell the
story of the youngest daughter of a gentleman in
Lincolnshire, which Shakespeare had long before
told of Signor Baptista, of Padua, the father of
" the curst shrew " whom Petruchio tamed. In
spite of this curious instance of gross ignorance, it
is abundantly clear that Shakespeare in his great
plays, even early in the eighteenth century, had
laid hold of the hearts of the people, or, at
all events, of the hearts of the playgoers. Pope,
who as a poet is as widely removed from him as
the north pole is from the south, speaks of him as
" justly and universally elevated above all other
dramatic writers. His poetry," he adds, " was
inspiration indeed ; he is not so much an imitator
as an instrument of nature ; and 'tis not so just to
say that he speaks from her as that she speaks
through him."   Richardson, who, like Pope, was

5

born in the seventeenth century, makes his
heroine, Miss Byron, on her arrival in London,
write to her friend : " If you find that I prefer the
opera itself—well as I love music—to a good play
of our favourite Shakespeare, then, my Lucy, let
your heart ache for your Harriet." Horace Walpole, who, as a boy of ten, had knelt down and
kissed the hand of George I., and who is often
looked upon as a bundle of clever affectations, in
one of his " Letters" speaks of "all my enthu-
siasm for Shakespeare." Gibbon, who was born
early in the reign of George II., and who entered
Magdalen College 139 years ago, recounts how
at Lausanne, on the Lake of Geneva, where he
spent nearly five of the years of his youth, he was
allowed to attend the little theatre which Voltaire
had set up there for the performance of his own
plays. " The habits of pleasure," he continues,
" fortified my taste for the French theatre, and
that taste has perhaps abated my idolatry for the
gigantic genius of Shakespeare, which is inculcated
from our infancy as the first duty of an Englishman." This idolatry Mrs. Barbauld thus mentions
in one of her letters written in 1776: " I am of
your opinion that we idolize Shakespeare rather
too much for a Christian country." [1]

[1] Pope's " Preface to Shakespeare"; "Sir Charles Grandi-

It had been by those who frequented the theatres that Shakespeare had been first worshipped. The fewness of the editions of his works that were printed in the first hundred years after his death is a convincing proof that he had no great popularity among readers. Early in the eighteenth century, as I have shown, a great change had set in. He was to pass from the stage to the library, and from the library to the parlour.

I would turn aside to attack for a moment the foolish vanity of some of the Germans, who impudently assert that their nation was the first to discover Shakespeare's genius, and that they showed us Englishmen how vast was the treasure which, as it were, had lain hidden in our soil, just as strangers from across the sea were the first to discover the gold reefs which had escaped the notice of the stupid savages of Australia. When as yet there was scarcely an Englishman who could read a line of German, except one or two courtiers who had learnt it in the hope of winning the favour of George I., and one religious enthusiast who had resolved to study in the original the works of the mystic shoemaker, Jacob Behmen, two

son," ed. 1754, i. 24 ; Walpole's " Letters," ix. 124 ; Gibbon's " Miscellaneous Works," i. 104 ; Mrs. Barbauld's " Works," ii. 14.

Englishmen, who almost in succession were at the head of the world of letters, as no two Englishmen have ever been since their time—Alexander Pope and Samuel Johnson—brought out editions of his works. As a rival in their labours, and coming between them in point of time, we find Warburton, whose name, if it is now well-nigh forgotten, was amongst the foremost in the middle of last century. It was Lessing, says Carlyle, who by "his 'Dramaturgie' first exploded the pretensions of the French Theatre, and with irresistible conviction made Shakespeare known to his countrymen." But the "Dramaturgie" was not published till 1767-8, just one hundred years after Dryden had declared that "Shakespeare was the man who of all modern and perhaps ancient poets had the largest and most comprehensive soul." It may indeed be the case that Lessing, as Coleridge maintains, "first proved to all thinking men—even to Shakespeare's own countrymen—the true nature of his apparent irregularities"—those deviations from the models of the Greek dramas which Corneille and Racine had so servilely followed.[1] But Lessing was only carrying further what Dryden and Johnson had begun. Dryden, in the preface

[1] Carlyle's "Miscellaneous Essays," i. 37; Coleridge's 'Biographia Literaria," p. 275.

to that fine play, " All for Love; or the World
Well Lost," so early as the year 1678, had attacked
those critics " who wholly form their judgments by
the French poets. For my part," he says, " I
desire to be tried by the laws of my own country ;
for it seems unjust to me that the French should
prescribe here till they have conquered. . . . Their
heroes are the most civil people breathing, but
their good-breeding seldom extends to a word of
sense. All their wit is in their ceremony ; they
want the genius which animates our stage ; and,
therefore, 'tis but necessary, when they cannot
please, that they should take care not to offend.
But as the civillest man in the company is commonly the dullest, so these authors, while they are
afraid to make you laugh or cry, out of pure good
manners make you sleep." Johnson, moreover, two
or three years before Lessing wrote, had ridiculed
the charge brought against Shakespeare that he
had neglected " those laws which have been insti-
tuted and established by the joint authority of
poets and of critics. To the unities of time and
place," he continues, " he has shown no regard ;
and perhaps a nearer view of the principles on
which they stand will diminish their value, and
withdraw from them the veneration which, from
the time of Corneille, they have very generally

received, by discovering that they have given more trouble to the poet than pleasure to the auditor."

Addison also in an Essay which he wrote when Johnson was a little child, says : " Our inimitable Shakespeare is a stumbling-block to the whole tribe of these rigid critics. Who would not rather read one of his plays, where there is not a single rule of the stage observed, than any production of a modern critic where there is not one of them violated ? " Yet it was Addison's own play which led Voltaire to "express his wonder that Shakespeare's extravagancies are endured by a nation which has seen the tragedy of Cato." [1] Lessing's criticism may have gone far deeper than Dryden's and Johnson's, but it was by English writers that Shakespeare's defence was first undertaken, and it was by the English people that the transcendency of his genius was first maintained. How ignorant we were of German, even at the close of last century, is shown in the preface to the translation of " The Sorrows of Werter," published in London in 1794. By that time Goethe was thirty-five years old, and had written four of his plays. The translator, speaking of him . as " Mr. Goethe,"

[1] Johnson's " Works," v. 118, 126 ; *The Spectator*, No. 592.

describes him in a footnote as "Doctor of Civil Law and author of some dramatic pieces which are much esteemed."

There was, indeed, one famous critic who, though he gloried in being born a Briton, was a German by origin, and a master of the German tongue— His Majesty, King George III. His criticism on Shakespeare, though it was not published till after his death, is, I suppose, one of the earliest made by any one who was skilled in both languages. Justice to the Germans will not allow me to pass it over in silence. "Was there ever," he cried to Miss Burney, "such stuff as great part of Shakespeare? Only one must not say so! But what think you? What? Is there not sad stuff? What? What?"

"Yes, indeed, I think so, sir, though mixed with such excellencies that—"

"Oh!" cried he, laughing good-humouredly, "I know it is not to be said! but it's true. Only it's Shakespeare, and nobody dare abuse him." [1]

There was a far greater man than George III.— a man neglected by him when he set up as the patron of literature— who seems to have been insensible to Shakespeare's genius. There is a touch of scorn when Oliver Goldsmith makes

[1] Madame D'Arblay's "Diary," ii. 398.

"the whole conversation run," in the Vicar of
Wakefield's parlour, "upon high life and high-
lived company, with pictures, taste, Shakespeare,
and the musical glasses." In his "Enquiry into
the Present State of Polite Learning" his contempt
is still more openly shown. There, speaking no
doubt of the plays 'which Garrick was bringing
back to the stage he says: "Old pieces are
revived, and scarcely any new ones admitted . . .
the public are again obliged to ruminate over
those hashes of absurdity, which were disgusting
to our ancestors even in an age of ignorance. . . .
We seem to be pretty much in the situation of
travellers at a Scotch inn; vile entertainment is
served up, complained of, and sent down; up
comes worse and that also is changed, and every
change makes our wretched cheer more unsavoury.
What must be done? Only sit down contented,
cry up all that comes before us, and admire even
the absurdities of Shakespeare. . . . In fact, the
revival of those pieces of forced humour, far-
fetched conceit, and unnatural hyperbole which
have been ascribed to Shakespeare is rather
gibbeting than raising a statue to his memory." [1]
It may, however, be the case that this censure was

[1] "The Vicar of Wakefield," chap. x. ; "An Enquiry,"
chap. xii.

due not altogether to bad taste and imperfect sympathies. Goldsmith unhappily, with all his fine qualities, was a man too much subject to envy. He was, perhaps, jealous of the homage paid to the mighty dead. He owned indeed to Horace Walpole that he envied Shakespeare. "Fame," we are told, "he considered as one great parcel, to the whole of which he laid claim. Whoever partook of any part of it, whether dancer, singer, sleight-of-hand man, or tumbler, deprived him of his right." He too had suffered from neglect. "Whenever I write anything," he once said, "the public make a point to know nothing about it." One of his comedies was refused by Garrick and the other by Colman.[1]

In the praise that was so liberally bestowed, and bestowed without ridicule, on Mrs. Montagu's silly essay, we see that there were others besides George III. and Oliver Goldsmith by whom Shakespeare's full greatness was not recognized. She did not hesitate to say at one time that "she trembled for Shakespeare," and at another time that "she was a little jealous for poor Shakespeare." The admiration excited by her dull and pompous

[1] Walpole's "Letters," vi. 379; Northcote's "Life of Reynolds," i. 248; Boswell's "Life of Johnson," iii. 252, 320.

Essay might raise not only our surprise but even
our contempt for the understanding of our forefathers, had we not seen the stir which has been
made by the silly fellow from over the Atlantic
with his nonsense about Bacon. Mrs. Montagu,
let us do her the justice to admit, did pack her
nonsense into a book so small that it can be read
at a sitting ; while he has swollen his to a bulk
that might with great advantage be used in any
well-regulated prison as a severe form of punishment in the case of all prisoners of intelligence.

In spite, however, of the evidence that is afforded
by George III., Goldsmith, and the patronage of
Mrs. Montagu, it is certain that even somewhat
early in last century Shakespeare's fame over-
shadowed all other English writers. Yet it had
taken the dull old world the best part of a hundred
years before it discovered his genius in all its
breadth and length and depth and height. Had
this lecture been given in the days of the Restoration or even a little later, it is quite possible that
his name and works might have been passed over
in silence, and that the omission might have been
scarcely noticed by the audience. In 1690, Sir
Thomas Blount published a work in which he had
collected the judgments passed by learned men on
the most famous writers of all ages. Among these

famous writers are not found Spenser, Shakespeare and Milton.

In every part of literature we discover the vast and sometimes very rapid changes that take place in literary taste. Let those who foretell immortality for Charlotte Bronté and George Eliot meditate on the fate that has come upon Fanny Burney. The men who admired her were greater than those who admired these two novelists of our day. Johnson not only read her stories with delight, but, as it were, acted them in his playful talk at the Thrales' house at Streatham. There were passages in " Evelina," he said, which might do honour to Richardson. Sir Joshua Reynolds sat up all night to finish it. When Boswell mentioned to Johnson her novel of " Cecilia," " sir," said he, " with an air of animated satisfaction, if you talk of ' Cecilia,' talk on." The book came out just as Mrs. Siddons became famous, and both women were the talk of the day. Johnson, at one of the gay assemblies of the Hon. Miss Monckton,—that lively lady famous for having at her house " the finest *bit of blue* "— Johnson, I say, exclaimed : " How these people talk of Mrs. Siddons ! I came hither in full expectation of hearing no name but the name I love and pant to hear, when from one corner to another they are talking of that jade, Mrs. Siddons! till, at last wearied out, I went yonder into a corner, and repeated to myself Burney! Burney! Burney! Burney!" " Ay, sir," said Mr. Metcalf, " you should have carved it upon the trees." " Sir, had there been any trees, so I should ; but there being none, I was content to carve it upon my heart." [1]

Mrs. Siddon's fame, I may remark, is still fresh ; but it is quite possible that her style of acting would be called stilted or conventional by a modern audience, and that she is chiefly praised because she is unknown. Had not a single copy of Miss Burney's novels been preserved, we might be mourning over that youthful female genius who kept some of England's greatest men from their work and their sleep. For the admiration of Johnson and Reynolds was shared by their great contemporaries. Gibbon boasted that he had read the whole of the five volumes of " Cecilia " in a day. " 'Tis impossible," cried Edmund Burke ; " it cost me three days, and you know I never parted with it from the day I first opened it." Even Horace Walpole, who was out of harmony with so many of the best writers of his age, read

---

[1] Madame D'Arblay's " Diary," i. 57 ; ii. 196-7 ; Boswell's " Life of Johnson," iv. 223.

it through, though he found it immeasurably long. He admitted that it had, with all its faults, "a thousand beauties." [1]

How splendid is the tribute paid by the author of the " Decline and Fall of the Roman Empire " to Henry Fielding. " Our immortal Fielding was of the younger branch of the Earls of Denbigh, who draw their origin from the Counts of Habsburgh, ·the lineal descendants of Eltrico, in the seventh century, Duke of Alsace. Far different have been the fortunes of the English and German divisions of the family of Habsburgh : the former, the knights and sheriffs of Leicestershire, have risen slowly to the dignity of a peerage ; the latter, the Emperors of Germany and Kings of Spain, have threatened the liberty of the Old, and invaded the treasures of the New World. The successors of Charles V. may disdain their brethren of England ; but the romance of ' Tom Jones,' that exquisite picture of human manners, will outlive the palace of the Escurial, and the imperial eagle of the House of Austria." Yet Johnson called Henry Fielding a blockhead, a barren rascal ; though he owned that he had read his novel of " Amelia " at a sitting. Richardson, Fielding's

[1] Madame D'Arblay's " Diary," ii. 127 ; Walpole's " Letters," viii. 285, 508.

great rival, had only been able to get through the first volume ; "for I found," he writes, "the characters and situations so wretchedly low and dirty that I imagined that I could not be interested for any one of them."[1] But Richardson, no doubt, was influenced by jealousy and resentment, though it must be admitted that even with the best goodwill he would have found it hard to discover much to admire in a writer who in sentiment was as far apart from him as a man well could be. When we come to examine into Gibbon's prophecy for Fielding of undying fame, we are forced to own that that great novelist is much more known than read. He who outside the society of men of letters alludes to any incident in his stories is little likely to be understood. His strange medley of innkeepers and their wives, excisemen, attorneys, doctors, parsons, squires, lieutenants, recruiting sergeants, lady's maids, beaus, fine ladies, rakes, keepers of prisons, gamblers, bailiffs, have well-nigh passed across the stage, and found their final exit. If I could believe that it was the profligacy of his writings which had brought about this change, then there

---

[1] Gibbon's "Miscellaneous Works," i. 4 ; Boswell's " Life of Johnson," ii. 174 ; Richardson's " Correspondence," iv. 60.

might be some cause for rejoicing. For profligate they undoubtedly were, though they were read by three of the purest-minded women of their age— Hannah More, Fanny Burney, and Anna Lætitia Barbauld. But I see lying on drawing-room tables novels which are ten times as corrupting as Henry Fielding's worst. If far too often he weakened the delicacy of the moral sense, yet he had a true eye for moral beauty. In his Amelia, his Sophia Western, he has given us women of the most beautiful purity and loveliness of character. But grievous though his failings were, he did not add one more to them. He never degrades the intellect. In his writings there is no intellectual corruption. " They have salt enough to keep them sweet, wit enough to preserve them from putrefaction." I could wish to see no young girl read " Tom Jones," or even " Joseph Andrews," though in it is enshrined that first of all English parsons, the simple, high-minded, learned, and most slovenly priest, Mr. Abraham Adams. But I would rather see her read Fielding, who would teach her much that is good, who would train her in wit and in the knowledge of some of the best qualities of the heart, than the works of many modern female novelists, who are popular though they are a disgrace to their sex; whose

views of life are as low and base as the style in
which they write, and as inaccurate as their
English ; and who have neither wit, nor humour,
nor sense, nor learning, nor knowledge, to throw
into the scale as a balance to the vast weight of
unworthy qualities which they have heaped up on
the other side. The day will come, I trust, when
our descendants, purified by some nobler strain of
thought, will look back upon many of the favourite
novelists of this age, male as well as female, as
men looked back upon the evil days of the
Restoration. The work will have to be done over
again which Addison did for the men of his time,
whose praise Johnson has celebrated in the following fine passage :

" It is justly observed by Tickell that Addison
employed wit on the side of virtue and religion.
He not only made the proper use of wit himself,
but taught it to others ; and from his time it has
been generally subservient to the cause of reason
and of truth. He has dissipated the prejudice
that had long connected gaiety with vice, and
easiness of manners with laxity of principles. He
has restored virtue to its dignity, and taught
innocence not to be ashamed. This is an elevation
of literary character 'above all Greek, above all
Roman fame.' No greater felicity can genius attain

than that of having purified intellectual pleasure, separated mirth from indecency, and wit from licentiousness ; of having taught a succession of writers to bring elegance and gaiety to the aid of goodness ; and, if I may use expressions yet more awful, of having 'turned many to righteousness.' " 1

The task of the future reformer will be not a little different and perhaps somewhat harder. " The wits of Charles," corrupt though they were, were corrupt wits. They stimulated even though they debased the mind. They gave it a quickness, an alertness, which might be turned to better ends. But the novelists of whom I am speaking deaden every part of the intellect. They are dull themselves and the cause of dulness in others. They leave those who largely indulge in them intellectually unfit for any work which requires sustained thought. They are the dram-shop keepers of the world of letters.

1 Johnson's " Works," vii. 451.

LECTURE III.

and admired by distant nations, there was a greater
likelihood of his being understood and admired by
distant ages. Now Fielding was little read on the
Continent. "The foreigners," said a traveller of
the time, "have no notion of his books, and do not
understand them, as the manners are so entirely
English." It is true that a French writer complained that the Anglomania was gaining on his
countrymen. "After 'Gulliver' and 'Pamela' here
comes 'Tom Jones,' and they are mad for him." [1]
The madness, however, neither extended far nor
lasted long.

When we turn to Fielding's great rival, Richardson, we find at all events that outward sign of
future fame. The novels of the awkward, vain,
middle-aged English bookseller spread rapidly
from land to land. I have seen an autograph
letter written to David Hume by the Marquis of
Mirabeau, *l'ami du peuple*, as he was called, the
father of the great Mirabeau, in which he says that
Richardson alone, the man in his eyes of the
greatest worth, made him often regret his ignorance
of English. Grimm, the great critic, seems to rank
him with Homer, Sophocles, and Raphael. Johnson's admiration of him was very great. He was

[1] "Letters of Mrs. Calderwood," p. 208 ; Jusserand's
"English Novel," p. 24.

LECTURE III.

I HAVE been led far away from the judgment
which some of the first men of the last century
passed on Fielding. Surely we ought to look upon
our own decisions as full of uncertainty when we
find two such men as Johnson and Gibbon wide as
the poles asunder in their criticisms on their famous
contemporary. The barren rascal, the blockhead
of one man will, says the other, outlive the palace
of the Escurial and the imperial eagle of the house
of Austria. There was one early indication that
Fielding did not merit the proud title that was
conferred on him of the Prose Homer of Human
Nature. It has been justly observed that distance
has somewhat the same effect as time in the
estimate which we form of authors—an effect,
however, which is rapidly lessening with the
increasing facilities of communication, and the
mingling of nations. If a writer was understood

one of the few men "whom he sought after."
"There is," he said, "more knowledge of the heart
in one of his letters than in all 'Tom Jones.'"
When the Hon. Thomas Erskine, afterwards the
famous Lord Chancellor, objected : "Surely, sir,
Richardson is very tedious," Johnson replied,
"Why, sir, if you were to read Richardson for the
story, your impatience would be so much fretted
that you would hang yourself. But you must read
him for the sentiment, and consider the story as
only giving occasion to the sentiment." Lord
Chesterfield, "the undisputed sovereign of wit and
fashion," said of him : "To do him justice he
never mistakes nature, and he has surely great
knowledge and skill both in painting and in
interesting the heart." Horace Walpole, I must
admit, spoke of him as one "who wrote those
deplorably tedious lamentations, 'Clarissa' and
'Sir Charles Grandison,' which are pictures of high
life as conceived by a bookseller, and romances
as they would be spiritualized by a Methodist
teacher." But Walpole had not the world with
him, above all, he had not the foreign world with
him. "Clarissa" was "one of the most popular
books in the German language," its two rivals
being Young's "Night Thoughts" and Hervey's
"Meditations among the Tombs." According

to Coleridge, it greatly influenced Schiller's
" Robbers." Fifty years after the great novelist's
death, Mrs. Barbauld, no mean critic, while ad-
mitting that " his works were not found to be so
attractive to the present generation as they were to
the past," added : " His fame stands higher abroad
than it does at home. He is as highly valued by
foreigners as Rousseau is by us ; and whatever be
his defects, his intrinsic merit is too great not to
place him above the varying taste of the day.
When a hundred novels that are now read are
passed away and forgotten, " Clarissa " will hold
its place among those standard works that adorn
the literature of our country." [1]

Jeremy Bentham describes how, in his childhood,
while staying at his grandmother's house in Berk-
shire, he " used to climb a lofty elm and read in its
branches. I was," he continues, " the more fond of
this while the labourers were thrashing corn in the
neighbourhood, as I was delighted to be in society
with which I was not compelled to mix. No
situation brought with it more felicity than to hide
myself in the tree, and having read for some time

---

[1] Sainte-Beuve's " Causeries de Lundi," vii. 311 ; Boswell's " Life of Johnson," ii. 174, iii. 314 ; Walpole's
" Letters," iv. 305 ; Coleridge's " Biographia Literaria," p.
276 ; Barbauld's edition of " Clarissa," vol. i. p. xlvi.

to descend to gather up wheat for the peasants to thrash, and then to mount again to my leafy throne." Among the books over which he pored was Richardson's famous novel. "'Clarissa' kept me day after day incessantly bathed in tears." [1] He would have done his own great work far more easily and quickly had he gone on feeding his imagination. He stifled it in himself and in his disciples too, training them to be rather reasoning machines than men and women. He forgot the lesson which he learnt in his leafy throne; he forgot the whispering wind, the rustling leaves, the swaying branch, the sound of the falling flail, all in delightful harmony with the words of the great master of the feelings; he put far from him gracefulness of language and tenderness of thought, and all that wins its way to the head through the heart. He struggled hard and long for man's welfare, but no words of his moved men to tears. He had no persuasiveness, and was not understood till he had found interpreters. That Richardson should thus have affected the founder of the Utilitarian Philosophy is indeed a striking proof of his power.

When those who were in their infancy when the author of "Clarissa" died had now, if they survived, reached man's limit of fourscore, Macaulay

[1] Bentham's "Works," x. 22.

in his famous speech on copyright said of him in the House of Commons : " No writings have done more to raise the fame of English genius in foreign countries. No writings are more deeply pathetic. No writings, those of Shakespeare excepted, show more profound knowledge of the human heart." Thackeray has described to us the great historian's admiration of the famous novelist. " I spoke to him once about ' Clarissa.' " "Not read 'Clarissa'!" he cried out. " If you have once read ' Clarissa,' and are infected by it, you can't leave it. When I was in India I passed one hot season in the Hills ; and there were the Governor-general, and the Secretary of Government, and the Commander-in-chief, and their wives. I had ' Clarissa ' with me ; and as soon as they began to read, the whole station was in a passion of excitement about Miss Harlowe and her misfortunes, and her scoundrelly Lovelace. The Governor's wife seized the book, the Secretary waited for it, the Chief Justice could not read it for tears." He acted the whole scene ; he paced up and down the Athenæum library. I dare say he could have spoken pages of the book : of that book, and of what countless piles of others." [1]　But Richardson has passed away.

[1] Macaulay's " Miscellaneous Works," ed. 1871, p. 615 ; Trevelyan's " Life of Macaulay," ed. 1877, i. 381.

Even so far back as my boyhood I remember
hearing wonder expressed when in company a lady
said that she had read " Sir Charles Grandison "
from beginning to end.   Since then there has been
a certain revival of interest in him—a revival due,
as most such revivals are, rather to students of
literature than to any change in the popular taste.
For one reader of his novels there are perhaps ten
readers of his rival's, neglected though Fielding is.

Of all the changes in literary taste, I know of
none more sudden and more striking than that
which brought Scotland, the Scotch language, and
the Scotch people into general popularity. Let
me read to you a passage, which, when I first read
it, led me to wonder almost as much as a traveller
might wonder who, returning to some spot in the
Western States of America, which a few years
before he had known as a wilderness, should find
there some large and thriving town. The writer
says : " The influence of Scottish associations, so
far as it is favourable to antiquity, is confined to
Scotchmen alone, and furnishes no resources to
the writer who aspires to a place among the
English classics. Nay, such is the effect of that
provincial situation to which Scotland is now
reduced, that the transactions of former ages are
apt to convey to ourselves exaggerated concep-

tions of barbarism, from the uncouth and degraded
dialect in which they are recorded." Now it was
no Englishman, no Southron, who wrote this.
They are the words of the famous Scotch professor, Dugald Stewart, in whom glowed the
perfervidum ingenium Scotorum. It was written
in a memoir of the Scotch historian, Robertson,[1]
and it was read before the Royal Society of Edinburgh. It was but nine years later that Walter
Scott published his " Lay of the Last Minstrel,"
and but eighteen years later that he published his
" Waverley." He may have been present when
this paper was read, for of this honourable Society
in later years he was the President. The blood
perhaps flowed faster in his youthful veins, as he
listened to these words, and his pulse beat quicker,
as he felt hidden powers stirring within him—
powers which should break through the narrow
bonds of mere locality, and extend " the influence
of Scottish associations," from one end of the wide
world to the other. Scott seems to me to have
answered the plaintive question, which only two
years before the " Lay of the Last Minstrel " was
written, was put by the great English poet as, in
his wanderings in the Highlands, he heard the
Solitary Reaper singing to herself—

[1] Page 185.

" Will no one tell me what she sings ?
Perhaps the plaintive numbers flow
For old, unhappy, far-off things,
And battles long ago :
Or is it some more humble lay,
Familiar matter of to-day ?
Some natural sorrow, loss, or pain,
That has been, and may be again."

Scott has told us all that the wandering poet had asked. He has told us of the

"unhappy far-off things
and battles long ago ; "

he has told us of

" Familiar matters of to-day,
Some natural sorrow, loss, or pain,
That has been, and may be again,"

and he has so told his tale that it is listened to by old and young, by rich and poor, by learned and unlearned, by all peoples, nations, and languages.

To him who has studied the history of the eighteenth century the change which he has wrought is indeed wonderful. Not only in England, but also in Lowland Scotland, the Highlanders in the days of our great-grandfathers were looked upon with a mixture of terror and contempt. When Johnson and Boswell in the country between Loch Ness and the western sea, in their mid-day halt, were surrounded by the M'Craas, "I observed to Dr. Johnson," Boswell records, "it was much the same as being with a tribe of Indians." "Yes, sir," replied Johnson, "but not so terrifying." " The villagers," writes Johnson, " gathered about us in considerable numbers, I believe without any evil intention, but with a very savage wildness of aspect and manner." Ray, in his "History of the Rebellion of 1745," speaks of the Young Pretender's army as "the barbarians that overrun the country." Hume, describing them " as a people who from the miserable disadvantages of their soil and climate were perpetually struggling with the greatest necessities of nature ; who from the imperfections of government lived in a continual state of internal hostility; ever harassed with the incursions of neighbouring tribes, or meditating revenge and retaliation on their neighbours "—Hume, I say, thus describing them, asks : " Have such a people leisure to think of any poetry, except perhaps a miserable song or ballad, in praise of their own chieftain, or to the disparagement of his rivals ? " Adam Smith, considering them as soldiers, says : "In point of obedience they were always much inferior to what is reported of the Tartars and Arabs. As, too,

from their stationary life they spend less of their
time in the open air, they were always less accustomed to military exercises, and were less expert
in the use of their arms than the Tartars and Arabs
are said to be." John Home, the dramatist, in the
year 1769 had written a tragedy on a Highland
story, and called it " Rivine." " The names of the
persons of the pieces," wrote Murphy, more than
thirty years later, "are grating to an English ear,
Kastreel, Dunton, Connon, and the like are exotics,
beneath the dignity of tragedy. The play might
as well be written in Erse. It was not fit to be
represented anywhere on this side of Johnny
Groats, at the remotest part of Scotland." " Garrick," says Dr. Alexander Carlyle, "justly alarmed
at the jealousy and dislike which prevailed at that
time against Lord Bute and the Scotch," had prevailed on Home " to change the title of ' Rivine'
into that of ' The Fatal Discovery,' and had provided a student of Oxford, who appeared at the
rehearsals as the author." [1]

How vast is the change in sentiment that has
been wrought since the days when a Highland

[1] Boswell's " Life of Johnson," v. 142 ; James Ray's
" History of the Rebellion of 1745," p. vii. ; Burton's " Life
of Hume," i. 479 ; "Wealth of Nations," ed. 1811, iii. 83 ;
Murphy's " Life of Garrick," p. 295 ; " Autobiography of Dr.
A. Carlyle," p. 509.

name was thought sufficient to damn a play. Now, not only Lowlanders, but even Englishmen, when they go to "the mountains of the North" are proud to disguise themselves in a dress which their forefathers in Edinburgh or in London would have looked on with a feeling of scorn not altogether unmingled with fear. Perhaps by the end of the twentieth century the descendants of the Orangemen of Belfast and Londonderry, and people of rank and fortune from England, when they go to shoot and fish in the wilds of Kerry or Connemara, will hope- in their long frieze coats, their knee-breeches, and their worsted stockings, to be taken for the children of the soil.[1] It was to Sir Walter Scott that this vast and most sudden change was greatly due. Something, no doubt, had been done by causes which I have not time to examine. But he was the mighty wizard of the north who waved his magic wand, and swept away the prejudices of men, and some of their sounder judgments too.

Dugald Stewart was by no means alone among Scotchmen in his contempt of "the uncouth and degraded dialect" of his forefathers. Hume, in his "History of England," describes how in the beginning of the Great Rebellion the chaplains of

[1] "Letters of D. Hume to W. Strahan," p. 62.

the Scottish Commissioners in London were run after by eager listeners. The church which had been assigned to them would not hold the multitudes of all ranks who crowded to it. "Those who were excluded," he continues, "clung to the doors or windows in hopes of catching at least some distant murmur or broken phrases of the holy rhetoric. All the eloquence of Parliament, now well refined from pedantry, animated with the spirit of liberty, and employed in the most important interests, was not attended to with such insatiable avidity as were these lectures, delivered with ridiculous cant, and a provincial accent full of barbarism and of ignorance." Beattie, a professor at Aberdeen, Burns's " sweet, harmonious Beattie," in his " Essays on Poetry and Music," speaking of what he calls "the vulgar broad Scotch," says : " To write in that tongue, and yet to write seriously, is now impossible ; such is the effect of mean expressions applied to an important subject ; so that if a Scotch merchant, or man of business, were to write to his countryman in his native dialect the other would conclude that he was in jest. Not that this language is naturally more ridiculous than others. But for more than half a century past it has even by the Scots themselves been considered as the dialect of the vulgar." Of

7

Ramsay's "Gentle Shepherd" he says: "To an Englishman who had never conversed with the common people of Scotland the language would appear only antiquated, obscure, or unintelligible; but to a Scotchman, who thoroughly understands it, and is aware of its vulgarity, it appears ludicrous, from the contrast between meanness of phrase and dignity or seriousness of sentiment."[1]   Ten years after the Aberdeen professor and poet had proclaimed to the world the degradation of his mother-tongue, there was printed in a little country town in the south-west of Scotland a small volume entitled "Poems, chiefly in the Scottish Dialect," by Robert Burns. If the "Cotter's Saturday Night" did not make Beattie blush for the wrong he had done his native language, he must indeed have been steeped in prejudice and affectation. His blushes could not undo the harm he had done. It was perhaps this very passage in his writings which led Burns in this noble poem suddenly to drop his natural dialect when he came to describe the reading of "the big Ha' Bible," and to take to English, in which he rarely moved with ease or grace.

Who with such examples before him of the in-

[1] Hume's "History of England," ed. 1773, vi. 385; Beattie's "Essays," ed. 1779, p. 381.

firmity of human foresight can be bold enough to forecast the future of literature ? Who, remembering Dugald Stewart's lament as a man of letters over "the provincial situation to which Scotland is now reduced," can forbear reflecting on the changes that may be wrought in the world of readers by one single man of commanding genius ? Surely these vast revolutions in literary taste which I have been describing—revolutions in which old favourites are pulled down and new favourites set up—will inspire us, if we are wise, with a great mistrust of our own judgment, and a great willingness to accept the judgment of the world, when it has stood the test of many generations. Yet such is the ardour with which in our youth we join ourselves, even in literature, to a party, that we are as unjust in our judgments as if we were nothing better than a set of mere politicians. If from pleasure we read those whom we admire, from a kind of ridiculous pride we abuse those of whom we know next to nothing. When I look back on my early years there are few things that I more regret than this ignorant partisanship. I was brought up among those whose canon of taste was contained in the *Edinburgh Review.* I sat, as it were, at the feet of Jeffrey and Macaulay. Not a doubt did I ever hear cast on their infallibility.

In them was contained all the law and the prophets. Byron's "English Bards and Scotch Reviewers" was constantly in the hands and on the tongues of my young associates. We learnt to laugh with the insolent poet at far better and far nobler men than himself. Wordsworth was our scoff. Yet I have the satisfaction of thinking that though it was against the faith in which I had been brought up, I could not help taking pleasure in "We are Seven," and the few simpler poems of his that I chanced to see. It is a pleasure to me now to reflect that I did not let slip the chance that I once had of seeing that great poet. When I was a boy of perhaps thirteen or fourteen I was told, as I was walking through Ambleside, that Mr. Wordsworth was just ahead in his chaise. I ran after him, and caught him up there where the old market-cross used to stand. He, I fancied, seeing a lad eagerly running and guessing what was in his heart, good-naturedly checked his horse and looked full round. I saw his venerable face, but I little knew at the time how dear he was to become to me.

I entered Oxford as ignorant of the new School of Poetry as any one well could be. I do not think that I had ever seen a single poem of Keats or Shelley. Mr. Browning's name was, I believe, un-

known to me. Of Wordsworth and Mr. Tennyson
I had read only a very few poems. Tennyson I
had heard treated with the same scorn as his great
forerunners. It was for me a most happy day
which first brought me within the influence of this
noble University, though the first experience was
bitter enough. The coat of ignorance and conceit
which had formed round me had to be stripped off,
and it had grown so close, that, in stripping, it
seemed to bring with it not a little of the skin.
When once more I began to breathe freely, I
exultingly owned that,

> " Largior hic campos æther et lumine vestit
> Purpureo ; Solemque suum, sua sidera norunt."

("Therein a more abundant heaven clothes all the meadows'
face
With purple light ; and their own sun and their own stars
they have.")

Let me here show how much in the happy
season of youth, when fresh forms are so easily
taken, when custom does not yet

> " lie upon us with a weight
> Heavy as frost and deep almost as life,"

how much in that bounteous time one friend can
do for another. It so chanced that in my second

term I every day sat at dinner in hall by a man very much my senior. In fact, shortly after I entered he took his Bachelor's degree. Something in my talk must, I suppose, have interested him. At all events he thought me worth taking in hand. He was, I remember, amused at the boldness, I might say the impudent audacity, of my literary judgments, and surprised, moreover, both at the extent and the narrowness of my reading. He proposed that he should come into my room every evening, and over a cup of tea should read with me the "In Memoriam." We went carefully through the whole poem, and by the end of it I belonged to the new school. So ardent an admirer did I become of its author, that I not only upheld his merit in our College Debating Society against a strong opposition, but scarcely had I taken my degree before, in the very village in which I had been brought up, at the very feet, as it were, of Gamaliel, in a lecture which I gave at the Mechanics' Institute, I boldly challenged for him a place among our great poets. Unhappily for me my friend had that failing of a literary apostle against which I have been warning you. He was so clear-sighted to the merits of the modern school that he was blind to the merits of that which it had supplanted. From him and his friends I learnt to speak of Pope with the same ignorant contempt as I had before spoken of Wordsworth and Tennyson. I went on to read Mr. Browning, and as my admiration for him increased, so increased my scorn for the poets who were of a widely different school. I think with grief of the time, the pleasure and the improvement which I have lost by this contempt of ignorance. He who refuses to read Pope loses, if nothing else, the delight that is given by perfect versification. " Sir," said Johnson, " a thousand years may elapse before there shall appear another man with a power of versification equal to that of Pope." Listen to the melody of these lines, which he wrote when he was but sixteen years old—" the marvellous boy" that he was, marvellous far than Chatterton.

> " No grateful dews descend from evening skies,
>   Nor morning odours from the flowers arise ;
>   No rich perfumes refresh the fruitful field,
>   Nor fragrant herbs their native incense yield.
>   The balmy zephyrs, silent since her death,
>   Lament the ceasing of a sweeter breath ;
>   The industrious bees neglect the golden store ;
>   Fair Daphne's dead, and sweetness is no more."

But there is far more than versification. Pope is a great poet, the greatest perhaps in his class,

though his class certainly is far below the highest.
Which of us is so rich in poetic thought that he
can venture to scorn those few lines in which he
describes the poor Indian's hope of finding

" Behind the cloud-topt hill an humbler heav'n ;'

or that noble passage in which speaking of the
Deity he says :—

" Who sees with equal eye, as God of all,
A hero perish, or a sparrow fall,
Atoms or systems into ruins hurl'd,
And now a bubble burst, and now a world."

Was the man no poet who asks

" Is it for thee the lark ascends and sings ?
Joy tunes his voice, joy elevates his wings.
Is it for thee the linnet pours his throat ?
Loves of his own and raptures swell the note."

As we study his perfect versification, we may
justly apply to him one of his finest couplets,

" The spider's touch, how exquisitely fine !
Feels at each thread, and lives along the line."

Pope's touch, exquisitely fine, does indeed seem
to live along almost every line which he wrote. In

his " Satires " and his " Moral Essays," " the position and choice of words," is surely, as Coleridge maintained, " almost faultless." [1] The more we study style, the more we train our ear to the melody of sentences and the sweetness of sound, the more we train our understanding to the precise use of words, the more shall we find to admire in Pope. We shall not, therefore, mistake his position as a poet, or assign to him a place in the first rank. He will still be far, immeasurably far below Shakespeare and Milton, but he will be among the first, if, indeed, he is not the very first, in the class to which he belongs. He is equal to Horace, and Horace has defied " the effacing fingers," of nearly two thousand years' decay. There are those who refuse to read him because his school of poetry is essentially artificial. He may be at the very top ; but top or bottom they will have none of it. Men who are far beneath him in the writer's art are more to their taste, if only they belong to a more natural school. They would more willingly consort with one who serves in heaven than with him who reigns in hell. Pope, it is true, if all his excellencies were increased a thousand-fold, would never be a step nearer to Shakespeare and Milton. The lofty and lonely heights on which they sit are

[1] " Biographia Literaria," p. 19.

separated by a great gulf from the pleasant hill to
which he has climbed; while far beneath them,
but still on the same range, are Wordsworth, Keats
and Shelley, Tennyson and Browning. The foolish
worshippers of Browning, indeed, in their wild
extravagance place him above Milton; but I will
not do them the injustice to believe that they have
ever read the " Paradise Lost." They are "shallow
in themselves," without being " deep-versed in
books." In the case of these five poets we could
conceive that, if their genius and their art had
been multiplied again and again, they might have
stood on "the starry threshold" by the side of
Milton, close before the throne of Shakespeare.
But though the poetry of even the lowest of the
five is far truer to nature than Pope's, yet his art
may be so much greater as to strike the balance.
Let me read to you what one of the masters of
their school says of the French tragedians. " However meanly I may think of their serious drama,
even in its most perfect specimens, the French
tragedies are consistent works of art, and the off-
spring of great intellectual power. Preserving a
fitness in the parts, and a harmony in the whole,
they form a nature of their own, though a false
nature. Still they excite the minds of the spectators to active thought, to striving after ideal

excellence." [1] That kind of excellence which can
be attained by a laborious study and practice of
style should surely be set before our eyes, for at
few times in the history of our country has slovenly
and eccentric writing more thriven than in these
latter days. We shall not take Pope as our model;
but we can, at least, be stirred up to strive after
ideal excellence by the perfection to which he
attained. Where can we find so many faultless
lines together as those famous two-and-twenty in
which he attacks Addison :

> " Peace to all such ! but were there one whose fircs
> True genius kindles, and fair fame inspires ;
> Bless'd with each talent and each art to please,
> And born to write, converse, and live with ease ;
> Should such a man, too fond to rule alone,
> Bear, like the Turk, no brother near the throne,
> View him with scornful, yet with jealous eyes,
> And hate for arts that caused himself to rise ;
> Damn with faint praise, assent with civil leer,
> And, without sneering, teach the rest to sneer ;
> Willing to wound, and yet afraid to strike,
> Just hint a fault, and hesitate dislike ;
> Alike reserved to blame or to commend,
> A timorous foe, and a suspicious friend ;
> Dreading e'en fools, by flatterers besieged,
> And so obliging that he ne'er obliged ;
> Like Cato, give his little senate laws,
> And sit attentive to his own applause ;

---

[1] Coleridge's " Biographia Literaria," p. 257.

> While wits and Templars every sentence raise,
> And wonder with a foolish face of praise—
> Who but must laugh, if such a man there be?
> Who would not weep, if Atticus were he?"

"Time," writes Johnson, "quickly puts an end to artificial and accidental fame; and Addison is to pass through futurity protected only by his genius."[1]   He is protected, too, by the genius of his enemy. It is impossible that this passage, perfect wit in perfect language, can ever be forgotten. As long as men read it they will seek to know more of this Atticus, and they will feel how stainless must have been the character of a man, how bright his wit, how delightful his writings, who sustained such an attack unhurt and untarnished. Pope, as he watched the effect of his blow at the reputation of his great rival, might well have exclaimed :

> " We do it wrong, being so majestical,
> To offer it the show of violence;
> For it is, as the air, invulnerable,
> And our vain blows malicious mockery."

Perfect as Pope is in satire, no less perfect is he in praise. In the same poem in which he attacks Addison, a few lines earlier he had thus celebrated his friends.

[1] Johnson's " Works," vii. 451.

" Why did I write ? what sin to me unknown
Dipp'd me in ink, my parents', or my own ?
As yet a child, nor yet a fool to fame,
I lisp'd in numbers, for the numbers came ;
I left no calling for this idle trade,
No duty broke, no father disobey'd :
The muse but served to ease some friend, not wife,
To help me through this long disease, my life ;
To second, Arbuthnot, thy art and care,
And teach the being you preserved to bear.
  But why then publish ? Granville the polite,
And knowing Walsh, would tell me I could write ;
Well-natured Garth inflamed with early praise,
And Congreve loved, and Swift endured my lays ;
The courtly Talbot, Somers, Sheffield read,
E'en mitred Rochester would nod the head,
And St. John's self (great Dryden's friends before)
With open arms received one poet more."

The greatest monarch could not confer such
honours as these. What was Lewis XIV. among
his courtiers in the great gallery of Versailles, what
was Napoleon at the Tuileries among the marshals
of France, bestowing titles and ribands and crosses,
compared with the sickly crook-backed dwarf thus
decorating his friends? As we read the lines we
seem to be passing through some lofty hall hung
with portraits by Vandyck. How poor was the
coronet given to St. John by the Queen, when set
side by side with the honours which Pope was
never tired of heaping on his friend ! The blue

riband of the Garter should have seemed worthless
to the man to whom the poet had written those
four lines unsurpassed for the splendour of the
compliment :

> " Oh ! while along the stream of time thy name
> Expanded flies, and gathers all its fame ;
> Say, shall my little bark attendant sail
> Pursue the triumph, and partake the gale ? '

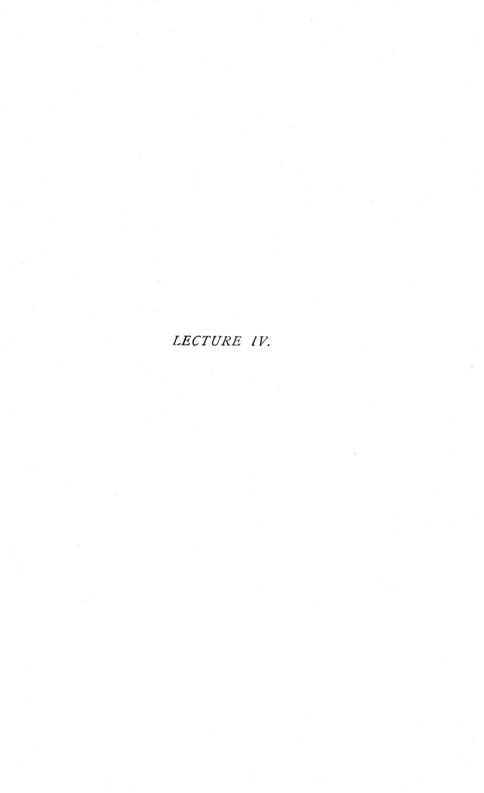

LECTURE IV.

LECTURE IV.

GREAT DRYDEN" himself, the poet of

"The varying verse, the full resounding line,
The long majestic march and energy divine,"

the "glorious John" of our forefathers, lies in even
deeper neglect than Pope. Yet his genius was
probably greater, though his art was certainly less.
I know of few more manly writers. The reader who
has nourished himself on his vigorous genius, and his
strong common-sense, supported and set forth as
they are by his learning, will have little relish for
weak fancy and mere tricks of language. What
Dryden might have done had he been as careful in
his workmanship as Pope we can only imagine. He
rose to heights above the younger poet's flight, but
in his careless haste he often sank far beneath him.
When he puts forth all his strength how great is
he! Who can read unmoved his "Songs for St.
Cecilia's Day"? They rouse us as soldiers are

8

roused by the sound of the trumpet. He was daring enough—and daring never went to greater heights—to do once more what Shakespeare had already done pre-eminently well, and to tell a second time the story of Antony and Cleopatra. He knew his strength, and he has not failed. Shakespeare's play perhaps ranks next, and only next, to the four great tragedies, " Hamlet," " Macbeth," " King Lear," and " Othello." Nevertheless, Dryden's " All for Love, or the World Well Lost," even though we have the echo of the other ever in our ear, is a great performance. How noble is the passage where Antony, in an outburst of shame, confesses his fault :

```
" ANTONY.        I have been a man, Ventidius.
VENTIDIUS.   Yes, and a brave one ; but—
ANTONY.      I know thy meaning.
             But, I have lost my reason, have disgraced
             The name of soldier with inglorious ease.
             In the full vintage of my flowing honours
             Sate still, and saw it pressed by other hands.
             Fortune came smiling to my youth and woo'd
                it,
             And purpled greatness met my ripened years.
             When first I came to empire I was borne
             On tides of people, crowding to my triumphs;
             The wish of nations ; and the willing world
             Received me as its pledge of future peace ;
             I was so great, so happy, so beloved,
             Fate could not ruin me ; till I took pains
```

And worked against my fortune, chid her
    from me,
And turned her loose ; yet still she came
    again.
My careless days and my luxurious nights
At length have wearied her, and now she's
    gone,
Gone, gone, divorced for ever."

How beautiful are the closing lines when the
Priest of Isis, before the dead bodies of Antony
and Cleopatra, exclaims :

" Sleep, blest pair,
Secure from human chance long ages out,
While all the storms of fate fly o'er your tomb."

How fine are the lines in " The Hind and the
Panther," in which Dryden justifies, or attempts to
justify, his conversion to the Church of Rome :—

" What weight of ancient witness can prevail,
  If private reason hold the public scale ?
  But, gracious God, how well dost thou provide
  For erring judgments an unerring guide !
  Thy throne is darkness in the abyss of light,
  A blaze of glory that forbids the sight ;
  Oh, teach me to believe Thee thus concealed,
  And search no farther than Thyself revealed ;
  But her alone for my director take,
  Whom Thou hast promised never to forsake !
  My thoughtless youth was winged with vain desires ;
  My manhood, long misled by wandering fires,
  Followed false lights ; and when their glimpse was gone,
  My pride struck out new sparkles of her own.

Such was I, such by nature still I am ;
Be thine the glory, and be mine the shame !
Good life be now my task ; my doubts are done ;
What more could fright my faith, than three in one?"

Such writings as these we surely cannot afford
to neglect, though they are cast in a mould which
has been long broken and thrown on one side. I
remember hearing a story told of a humorous old
painter who was visited in his studio by a young
gentleman fresh from a tour in Italy. "I have been
to Italy," said the young man, "and, to tell you the
truth, I don't see much in it." His old friend went
on quietly painting, saying in a low tone, as if to
himself, "Poor devil! Been to Italy! Does not
see much in Italy! Poor devil!" Well, I must
confess that in my undergraduate days contempt
of Dryden and Pope I was almost as poor a devil
as the young gentleman fresh from Italy. In truth
we are most of us, at one time or other of our lives,
so many Dogberrys in point of literature. We are
proud of our losses. We boast, not only that we
have two gowns and everything handsome about
us, in other words, that we can see the beauties of
Shelley and Browning, but that we have had losses,
in other words, that we have no pleasure in Dryden
and Pope. I have known a lad proud of never
eating apple-pie. We all know the air with which

a young man, who is free by a year or two from the temptations of the toffee-shop, announces to his hostess at dinner the important fact that he never eats sweets. If we are to indulge in this affectation, let us confine it to the table, and not let it spread to our bookshelves. Let us never forget that every writer who has stood the test of time must have in him something good, and almost certainly has something great. If we cannot discover it, let us not be unwilling to own to ourselves that it is in ourselves, and not in him, that the fault lies. He who has learnt to enjoy a great writer, or a school of great writers, to whose beauties he was before insensible, has opened for himself a fresh inlet of happiness, and has enlarged the borders of his understanding. Let me illustrate this by an interesting passage from Sir George Trevelyan's Life of his uncle, Lord Macaulay.

" Macaulay had a very slight acquaintance with the works of some among the best writers of his own generation. He was not fond of new lights, unless they had been kindled at the ancient beacons ; and he was apt to prefer a third-rate author, who had formed himself after some recognized model, to a man of high genius, whose style and method were strikingly different from anything that had gone before. In books, as in people and places, he loved that, and that only, to which he had been accustomed from boyhood upwards. Very few among the students of Macaulay will have detected the intensity and in some cases, it must be confessed, the wilfulness, of his literary conservatism : for, with the instinctive self-restraint of a great artist, he permitted no trace of it to appear in his writings. In his character of a responsible critic, he carefully abstained from giving expression to prejudices in which, as a reader, he freely indulged. Those prejudices injured nobody but himself ; and the punishment which befel him, from the very nature of the case, was exactly proportioned to the offence. To be blind to the merits of a great author is a sin which brings its own penalty ; and, in Macaulay's instance, that penalty was severe indeed. Little as he was aware of it, it was no slight privation that one who had by heart the ' Battle of Marathon,' as told by Herodotus, and the ' Raising of the Siege of Syracuse,' as told by Thucydides, should have passed through life without having felt the glow which Mr. Carlyle's story of the charge across the ravine at Dunbar could not fail to awake even in a Jacobite ; that one who so keenly relished the exquisite trifling of Plato should never have tasted the description of Coleridge's talk in the ' Life of John Sterling ' ; that one who eagerly and minutely

studied all that Lessing has written on art, or
Goethe on poetry, should have left unread Mr.
Ruskin's comparison between the landscape of the
'Odyssey' and the landscape of the 'Divine
Comedy,' or his analysis of the effect produced on
the imagination by long continued familiarity with
the aspect of the 'Campanile' of Giotto."

Sir George Trevelyan, after thus forcibly pointing
out his famous uncle's losses, goes on to make
them of very little moment. He says :

" Great beyond all question, was the intellectual
enjoyment that Macaulay forfeited by his unwilling-
ness to admit the excellence of anything which had
been written in bold defiance of the old canons; but,
heavy as the sacrifice was, he could readily afford
to make it. With his omnivorous and insatiable
appetite for books there was, indeed, little danger
that he would ever be at a loss for something to
read." [1]

Is there, then, nothing but a loss of enjoyment
in such a state of mind as this ? Is that all the
sacrifice that was made ? Did Macaulay lose
nothing by not attempting to understand two
writers who have so deeply touched and even
changed the thoughts of men ? It is too early to
estimate the influence which Mr. Carlyle and Mr.

[1] " Life of Lord Macaulay," ii. 463.

Ruskin have exerted on their time. That can only be done by thinkers scarcely yet born ; but that their influence has been great, I might almost say vast, can hardly be denied. To all this influence, though it was working all around, Macaulay was insensible. It was his proud hope and noble ambition that he was writing for far distant ages. " I have aimed high," he writes, in speaking of his " History of England " ; " I have tried to do something that may be remembered ; I have had the year 2000, and even the year 3000 often in my mind. I have sacrificed nothing to temporary fashions of thought and style." Eight years later he wrote, just after the publication of the third and fourth volumes, "The victory is won. The book has not disappointed the very highly raised expectations of the public. The first fortnight was the time of peril. Now all is safe." [1] Surely when he wrote these triumphant words the far out-look on the distant centuries must have been closed to him for a time. He needed some Solon to read to him the lesson that was read to the Lydian King, and to tell him that between the years 1856 and 3000 there were 29,744 fortnights, " whereof not one but will produce events unlike the rest." Schools of style, of thought, of feeling, will rise and pass away, and time will go

[1] " Life of Lord Macaulay," ii. 247, 392.

on, as time ever has gone on, endlessly sifting the works of men, and casting on one side among the rubbish of the centuries much that is good, much that is beautiful, much even that bears the mark of high and noble genius, but which reflects too faithfully the age in which it was written, and too little the common feelings of all mankind. Had Macaulay been able to enter into the thoughts of men whose genius was eccentric as well as great ; who, to use Johnson's phrase, " delight to tread upon the brink of meaning," the shout of the first fortnight would, I believe, have been far less loud, but the echo might have rolled from age to age. For if anything is fatal to his fame, it will be this imperfect sympathy of his with men who did not, to use Carlyle's humorous phrase, agree with him in looking upon the Divine government of the world as a limited whig monarchy. Had he, in the vast sweep of his reading, been able with understanding and sympathy to study the works of writers to whom, by the constitution of his mind, he was most strongly opposed, then we might with good and reasonable hope have joined in the proud thought that men who are separated from us by a greater interval of time than we are separated from King Alfred, will delight in our great historian, who, with all his failings, is certainly one of the chief glories of his age. But I find few traces in his writings or his "Life" that he was aware of the need under which we all lie, of trying to understand those with whom by nature we are most at variance, and of trying by their perfections to piece our imperfections. "Unto the Jews a stumbling-block, and unto the Greeks foolishness" is a text that can be applied in literature as well as in religion. George Fox, the Quaker, was to Macaulay a stumbling-block and a foolishness, and so was James Boswell, and so even, in some respects, was Samuel Johnson. I can never read his famous article in the *Edinburgh Review* on Boswell's "Life of Johnson" without a feeling of amazement that, with all its brilliancy, it could have been written by a man who was thirty years of age. In its gross ignorance of human nature it was scarcely worthy even of a hopeful lad, a scholar of Balliol, or of Trinity College, Cambridge, in his freshman's year.

The temptations to which the clever young students of the present age are exposed are very different from those which beset our fathers and our grandfathers. There is no fear at present lest common sense should be set up as the image before which we are all to fall down and worship. The path which leads to the shrine of that deity seems likely to become a little grass-grown. In

a college common room in this university I
happened to observe that there never had been,
I believed, a time in which men who knew so
much wrote so ill. Every age, I said, has its
affectations, but the peculiarity of this age was,
that men of some learning—learning at all
events which had been decorated with high university distinctions, with first-classes, with prizes,
with fellowships—that men so distinguished often
wrote nonsense—flowery nonsense it might be, but
none the less nonsense. A young man in the
company replied that men now-a-days were so
much more subtle in their thoughts that language
failed them, and that it was not they, but the imperfections of our tongue that were at fault. It
may be so; but, nevertheless, I shall not easily be
persuaded that this English of ours which, in the
hands of so many mighty poets and thinkers and
writers of every style, has been a perfect and most
beautiful instrument, answering the master's touch,
whatever note he struck, however high or however
low, is too imperfect for these modern thinkers.
As we see Shakespeare play upon it we feel as
Jubal's brethren felt.

> " When Jubal struck the chorded shell,
> His listening brethren stood around,
> And wondering on their faces fell

To worship that celestial sound :
Less than a God they thought there could not dwell
Within the hollow of that shell,
That spoke so sweetly and so well."

And now this "chorded shell" is not good enough for our subtle thinkers! I see no such predominance of thought in my contemporaries as can justify the haze in which they are so often enveloped. He who thinks clearly writes clearly in all ages of the world. When I think of the redundancy and the folly of the words by which many of our popular writers seem both to give pleasure to their readers and to fill their own pockets, I can easily fancy that when they were launched into the world their Genius addressed them as the Host in the "Merry Wives of Windsor" addresses Bardolph, when he engages him as tapster: "Let me see thee froth and live." Surely these authors are the very tapsters of literature. Their whole art consists in serving up poor liquor with what is called, in the slang of the tavern bar, a head to it: they do indeed froth and live! How admirable, by the way, is Falstaff's indignation in the same play when he is mocked by Sir Hugh Evans! "Seese and putter! have I lived to stand in the taunt of one that makes fritters of English?" Fritters now-a-days are made of English by men who have not the excuse of the honest Welsh parson—men to whom "Chatham's language is their mother tongue,"—men who have studied letters in a great university.

There is, I suppose, scarcely a single age to be found in which the writers of all classes below the first are entirely free from affectation : " We not only think in track," as Goldsmith said ; but we write in track. Among "the depravations in the republic of letters " he places first "affectation in some popular writer leading others into vicious imitation." At the time when he wrote this there was setting in a vicious imitation of Johnson's style. A young student of Queen's College has left a curious account of the lectures given in Oxford in the year 1779 by Dr. Scott, at that time a Fellow of University College, and Professor of Ancient History, but afterwards the famous Judge of the Admiralty Court and Lord Stowell. " Scott is intimate with Dr. Johnson," the young student writes, " and has a good deal of his manner : elevated style, pointed antithesis, rounded periods, moral and penetrating remarks. Sometimes, however, he copies the Doctor's faults, such as his turgid expressions, and that care to avoid the mention of anything mean or familiar by its common name. This is a grand source of burlesque.

For how does a man stare when at the bottom of a
grand-sounding sentence he discovers what is as
well known to him by its usual appellation as his
gloves or his pocket handkerchief. This was
sometimes the case with our lecturer, when he
was forced to descend to familiar topics. He
turned, doubled, and practised all the windings of
a hunted hare, in order to avoid that odious word
butter or cheese, and talked with great ingenuity
about shoes for several minutes without naming
them. Describing the houses of the Athenians he
acquainted his audience 'that they had no con-
venience by which the volatile parts of fire could
be conveyed into the open air.' How would a
bricklayer stare at being told that he meant no
more than that the Athenians had no chimneys!
One great inconvenience attended this constant
and studied elevation, for whenever he popped
out a familiar word, for which it was impossible to
substitute a synonym, it came from him with as
ill a grace as an oath would from a bishop, or the
language of Billingsgate from a fine lady." [1] Johnson, I may remark, would not have hesitated for
one moment to call shoes, shoes, and a chimney a
chimney. He tells us of Milton's pipe of tobacco,

[1] Goldsmith's " Present State of Polite Learning," chap.
iv., xi. ; " Letters of Radcliffe and James," p. 92.

and of the silver saucepan to which Pope's death was imputed. He could call a spade a spade as well as any man.

More than twenty years after Dr. Scott had thus amused the undergraduates of Oxford, Dugald Stewart, the great rhetorical philosopher, gave his first course of lectures on Political Economy at Edinburgh. "It was not unusual," says one who was present, "to see a smile on the face of some when they heard subjects discoursed upon seemingly beneath the dignity of the academical chair. The word *corn* sounded strangely in the moral class, and *drawbacks* seemed a profanation of Stewart's voice." [1]

When at length the vicious imitation of Johnson's style ceased to be fashionable, the world was none the freer from affectation. Goldsmith would still have found a depravation in the republic of letters. One hundred years or so after he uttered his complaint most of the young authors were under the influence of a man as unlike Johnson in his style as he was like him in his sturdy independency, his fearlessness, his truthfulness, his rugged tenderness, and his natural piety—Thomas Carlyle. Now I would apply to Carlyle's style a passage in which Macaulay describes his own. "I

[1] Cockburn's "Memorials of his Time," p. 174.

looked," he records in his diary, "through ——'s two volumes. He is, I see, an imitator of me. But I am a very unsafe model. My manner is, I think, and the world thinks, on the whole a good one ; but it is very near to a very bad manner indeed, and those characteristics of my style which are most easily copied are the most questionable."[2] Whatever may be the merits of Carlyle's style— and that it has great merit most men allow, even those who most clearly see the great faults by which it is marred—it is certainly true of it also "that those characteristics which are most easily copied are the most questionable." Sir George Trevelyan regretted, as you have seen, that his uncle could not relish Carlyle's descriptive writings. Much as I have enjoyed them myself, I have been sometimes inclined to think that in the long run they have caused me more misery than pleasure. It was my fortune for many a year to be a Saturday Reviewer—one before whose judgment-seat passed a great variety of writers, most of them, I regret to say, criminals more or less guilty ; worthy if not of death, at least of stripes. I look back even now, when they trouble me no longer, with a kind of horror on the word-painters, as, I suppose,

[1] Mr. Froude, I conjecture.
[2] " Life of Lord Macaulay," ii., 456.

they may justly be called, for their worthless art is called word-painting.

Carlyle, with all the power of a great master, has described the field of Dunbar or "the beach of Kirkaldy in summer twilights, a mile of the smoothest sand, with one long wave coming on gently, steadily, and breaking in gradual explosion into harmless melodious white, at your hand all the way ; the break of it rushing along like a mane of foam, beautifully sounding and advancing." [1] Mr. Ruskin, lecturing at Edinburgh, thus brings before the mind's eye a distant city of Italy :

"Now I remember a city, more nobly placed even than your Edinburgh, which, instead of the valley that you have now filled by lines of railroad, has a broad and rushing river of blue water sweeping through the heart of it ; which, for the dark and solitary rock that bears your castle, has an amphitheatre of cliffs crested with cypresses and olive ; which, for the two masses of Arthur's Seat and the ranges of the Pentlands, has a chain of blue mountains higher than the haughtiest peaks of your Highlands ; and which, for your far-away Ben Ledi and Ben More, has the great central chain of the St. Gothard Alps : and yet as you go out of the gates, and walk in the suburban streets of that

[1] "Reminiscences of Thomas Carlyle," i. 104.

city—I mean Verona—the eye never seeks to rest on that external scenery, however gorgeous ; it does not look for the gaps between the houses, as you do here ; it may for a few moments follow the broken line of the great Alpine battlements ; but it is only where they form a background for other battlements, built by the hand of man. There is no necessity felt to dwell on the blue river or the burning hills. The heart and eye have enough to do in the streets of the city itself ; they are contented there ; nay, they sometimes turn from the natural scenery, as if too savage and solitary, to dwell with a deeper interest on the palace walls that cast their shade upon the streets, and the crowd of towers that rise out of that shadow into the depth of the sky." [1]

The art of Carlyle and Ruskin, because of its ease, seems easy ; and so a host of servile imitators spring up like mushrooms in a September night. Everything is described in the heavens above, or in the earth beneath, or in the waters under the earth, and is described at a length that justifies the suspicion that the payment, as indeed often is the case, is at the rate of penny-a-line more or less. Description runs mad, and vulgarly mad ; for the infinitely little and the infinitely base are painted

---

[1] " Lectures on Architecture and Painting," ed. 1855, p. 3.

with words as many and as fine as the beautiful and the sublime. How often, as I have toiled through the piled-up epithets, each substantive duly supported by its triplet of adjectives, and each verb by at least a brace of adverbs, while the writer is painting perchance the beginning of spring, have I called to mind the master-touches in which in two lines the poet does what these word-painters fail to do in twice two hundred:

> " He felt the cheering power of spring,
> It made him whistle, it made him sing."

Do we ask for a picture of a spring day? This single couplet at once brings the April in our eyes. Let me quote a passage from a writer who assuredly had very little observation of the face of nature, and whose powers of description were therefore small, to show you in how few words, when they are well chosen, a wild and striking scene may be brought before us. Dr. Johnson is describing his ride on a wild and stormy night of late autumn through the Highlands of Argyle.

" The wind was loud, the rain was heavy, and the whistling of the blast, the fall of the shower, the rush of the cataracts, and the roar of the torrent, made a nobler chorus of the rough music of nature than it had ever been my chance to hear before." [1]

What better description of a wild mountain ride could we have had even though the writer had heaped up his words as if he were piling Ossa on Pelion, and leafy Olympus on Ossa?

Goldsmith, in the humorous account which he gave to Sir Joshua Reynolds of the arrival of himself and his friends at Calais, says : " Upon landing two little trunks, which was all we carried with us, we were surprised to see fourteen or fifteen fellows all running down to the ship to lay their hands upon them ; four got under each trunk, the rest surrounded and held the hasps ; and in this manner our little baggage was conducted with a kind of funeral solemnity till it was safely lodged at the Custom-house." [2] Now the words of many of the modern descriptive writers bear much the same relation to the thoughts which they, as it were convey, as these Calais porters bore to the luggage.   There is a struggling procession of substantives, adjectives, verbs, and adverbs, all bustling along, knocking one against the other, tripping over one another's heels, stunning the ears with a confused din, bear-

---

[1] Southey's " Inchcape Bell " ; Johnson's "Works," ix. 155.

[2] Forster's " Life of Goldsmith," ed. 1871, ii. 216.

ing along in triumph a couple of empty band-boxes.
I have one great hope that this word-painting will
have but a brief existence, and "with all its trumpery" will pass away for ever. "'Tis," as Hamlet
says, "as easy as lying," and so can be practised
by every one. It is the kind of stuff that "a man
might write for ever, if he would abandon his
mind to it." Since then every man, every woman,
and every child can become his own word-painter,
the art must cease to be profitable. Moreover,
happily, in every case there does come at length a
surfeit of bad taste. The world may remain as
foolish as ever ; the common stock of folly may
keep as large as ever, whatever changes may take
place ; folly, as Horace Walpole says, may be
matter, and, therefore, cannot be annihilated ;
nevertheless, a change the world will have, even
though it is only a change of foolishness. It is
my hope, my confident hope, therefore, that from
word-painting the land will soon have rest ; if not
for ever, nevertheless, for a period far exceeding
in length the scriptural one of forty years. That
this blessed time may the sooner begin, let me beg
you one and all to make a vow of abstinence from
the use of the dozen or two of epithets with which
these word-painters mix all their colours. Try to
pass a whole twelvemonth without so much as

once writing, or even uttering, sheen and sheer, shimmer and subtle and weird and opalescent and glint and the rest. Your mothers and your grandmothers got through life comfortably enough without the use of any one of them. Do not have the reproach cast on you which was cast on the schoolmaster and the curate in "Love's Labour Lost"—"They have been at a great feast of languages and stole the scraps." Do not be content to live "on the alms-basket of words." Lay to heart the advice which Charles Lamb gave to a friend who had sent him his poems: "If you count," he wrote, "you will wonder how many times you have repeated the word *unearthly;* thrice in one poem. It is become a slang word with the bards ; avoid it in future lustily." [1]

There will also be before long, I trust, a return to that clearness of writing which was perhaps the most distinguishing mark of the writers of the eighteenth century — a clearness which was due mainly to clear thinking, but partly also to the trouble which they took to write clearly. Of style they made a careful and even a laborious study. "How little," wrote Macaulay more than forty years ago, "how little the all-important art of making meaning pellucid is studied now! Hardly any

[1] "Letters of Charles Lamb," ed. A. Ainger, ii. 107.

popular writer, except myself, thinks of it. Many seem to aim at being obscure. Indeed, they may be right enough in one sense, for many readers give credit for profundity to whatever is obscure, and call all that is perspicuous shallow. But coraggio! and think of A.D. 2850. Where will your Emersons be then? But Herodotus will still be read with delight. We must do our best to be read too." [1]

Macaulay often fell into the opposite error, and wrote too clearly, for he leaves nothing for his readers to do but understand him without the slightest exertion on their part. He never goes shares with them, to use Charles Lamb's expression. He writes like a skilled rhetorician who, when addressing an audience, does not hesitate to repeat himself, so long as he varies the words, knowing well that either through inattention or stupidity much of what he says would be otherwise lost. What may be a merit in a spoken speech is a defect in a written book. Macaulay's condescending clearness becomes at times very tedious. When we have once firmly grasped the fact that two and two make four, we do not care to be told that by the addition of two and two is composed the fourth numeral. The obscurity under which

[1] " Life of Lord Macaulay," ii. 273.

we are now suffering differs not a little from that of which Macaulay complained. The writers whom he attacked affected a depth of thought—German thought, if I may so term it—which in its own nature, they maintained, could not but be obscure. We have still, as I have shown, this pretence of thinking beyond the powers of clear utterance ; but added to it, we have a profusion of epithets— apparently often chosen at random, and pitched into the midst of the sentence for their picturesqueness, not for any meaning that they have or purpose that they serve.   At their best they are but

"Rich windows that exclude the light ;"

at their worst they are

"Passages that lead to nothing."

Even those authors who manage this modern style best fatigue by their very brilliancy.   A brilliant writer indeed tries poor human patience almost as much as a brilliant performer on the pianoforte. How good was the advice given by "the old tutor of a college to one of his pupils—"Read over your compositions, and wherever you meet with a passage which you think is particularly fine, strike it out."[1] But in this particular brilliant style which I am

[1] Boswell's "Life of Johnson," ii. 237.

attacking there is nothing but bright-coloured patches—nothing but shreds of *purpureus pannus* stitched together after the fashion of a coverlet that is made up by piecing together the gaudiest snippings, the gatherings of many years. Every thread of every patch is made as bright as the brightest. There is nothing but glare. I would as soon walk along the eastern bank of a stream in the late afternoon of an unclouded day in summer, and be distressed by the dazzling reflection of the sinking sun in the water as read such writers as these. There is no good to be got from them. To write fine passages, such as those which the old tutor told his pupil to strike out, may be a useful exercise ; for from the practice of rhetoric comes a facility of writing. I hold, indeed, that a young man gives not a little promise as a writer, who in the first draft often writes finely, but who in the revision has good taste enough to detect the tinsel, and courage enough to rip it off. But when all is brilliancy, then nothing can be cut away. The whole must go or nothing.

Nourished as I have chiefly been on writers of a very different school from those who are the favourites of the present day, I may see too clearly and attack too strongly the faults of a school which I detest. Nevertheless, I cannot be wrong when I

maintain that as every age of writers has faults, and
faults peculiar to itself, he who wishes to write well
must study writers of different ages and widely
different styles. A language, like a country in
unsettled times, is threatened on all sides with
constant invasions; but it has this great danger
added that the young recruits are too apt to turn
deserters, and not only to throw open the gates to
the invaders who are pouring in, but even to deck
themselves with their foreign badges. We are
often blinded, moreover, to that duty which we
owe to our noble language by some of our best
affections. We see so strongly the merits of some
great teacher that we refuse to see his faults.
" We cannot love without imitating," says Landor;
" and we are as proud in the loss of our originality
as of our freedom."[1] " I have such a love for Mr.
Ruskin," said an earnest student to a friend of
mine, "that even when I know that what he writes
is absurd, I do my best not to see it." "Amicus
Plato, sed magis amica veritas." Mr. Ruskin is
is doubtless dear, but truth should be still dearer.
The only safeguard against this excessive, this
superstitious hero-worship, is to be found in the
number and in the diversity of our heroes. He
who enjoys a great variety of styles is much less

[1] " Pericles and Aspasia," ed. by C. G. Crump, i. 69.

likely to fall into the faults of any single one.
Had we lived a hundred years ago, while we
studied in the "Rambler" or the "Lives of the
Poets" the force, the clearness, and the cadence
which had been given to our language by Johnson,
we should, if we were wise, have carefully guarded
ourselves against a mode of composition which was
essentially faulty, to whose fascinations, nevertheless,
some great writers yielded far too much. In fact,
we should have done well to follow Johnson's own
advice when he says that "whoever wishes to attain
an English style, familiar but not coarse, and elegant but not ostentatious, must give his days and
nights to the volumes of Addison."[1]

The advice which I am giving is, I am well
aware, by no means easy to follow. We have our
prejudices against us, and, as I have said, our
affections too. We do not easily mingle minds
with those from whom we are widely different. In
our youth we are hero-worshippers, and when age
begins to steal upon us the indolence of the growing
years whispers to us that the study of new schools
of thought is certainly hard, and not certainly profitable. Yet the effort must be made. Taste can
be ruined, and on the ruins of taste countless are
the evils which spring up and thrive.

[1] Johnson's "Works," vii. 473.

LECTURE V.

LECTURE V.

IN this lecture and my next I wish to examine the part which the study of literature should play in education. What is our chief, our highest aim I would ask, in the education which we give to the young, and which, if we are wise, we never cease to give to ourselves? It is a question to which a different answer is far too commonly given now from what was given of old. The world is looked upon as a vast battle-field in which the exceeding great reward is not the inner life nobly lived, but the outer life nobly recompensed. It is not a race against ourselves, but a race against outsiders. It is not a race where all who run, if they have laboriously trained themselves are sure of a prize, but one in which the runners are many and the prizes few. The child, the boy, the young man are not taught that their chief competitors are themselves. It is not themselves but their companions that they must strive to overcome. As if this strife were not enough we are terrified by the sound of foreign competition. Unless our children are taught the natural sciences, French and German, shorthand, and what not, we shall be beaten out of all the markets of the world. The laborious Germans have already supplanted us, we are told, in many a distant mart; the manufactures of England must dwindle away because our lads know nothing of chemistry, while the ignorance of our commercial travellers and clerks of modern languages will make the sun of England's glory set. The day will come before long when it will be said that:

> " She whom mighty nations curtsied to,
> Like a forlorn and desperate castaway
> Did shameful execution on herself,"

by her neglect of what is vulgarly known as the modern side. Such was not the view of education maintained by Samuel Johnson in that fine passage in which he criticizes Milton's scheme:

" But the truth is, that the knowledge of external nature, and the sciences which that knowledge requires or includes, are not the great or the frequent business of the human mind. Whether we provide for action or conversation, whether we

wish to be useful or pleasing, the first requisite is
the religious and moral knowledge of right and
wrong; the next is an acquaintance with the
history of mankind, and with those examples
which may be said to embody truth, and prove by
events the reasonableness of opinions. Prudence
and justice are virtues and excellencies of all times
and of all places; we are perpetually moralists,
but we are geometricians only by chance. Our
intercourse with intellectual nature is necessary;
our speculations upon matters are voluntary, and
at leisure. Physiological learning is of such rare
emergence, that one may know another half
his life, without being able to estimate his skill in
hydrostatics or astronomy; but his moral and
prudential character immediately appears.

"Those authors, therefore, are to be read at
schools that supply most axioms of prudence,
most principles of moral truth, and most materials
for conversation; and these purposes are best
served by poets, orators, and historians.

"Let me not be censured for this digression, as
pedantic and paradoxical; for, if I have Milton
against me, I have Socrates on my side. It was
his labour to turn philosophy from the study of
nature to speculations upon life; but the inno-
vators whom I oppose are turning off attention

from life to nature. They seem to think that we are placed here to watch the growth of plants, or the motions of the stars. Socrates was rather of opinion that what we had to learn was, how to do good and avoid evil.

" ὅττι τοι ἐν μεγάροισι κακόν τ'ἀγαθόν τε τέτυκται " [1]

I am very far from holding with Johnson in all that he says, as I shall presently show ; but this I do hold, that whether we are dealing with the child of a ploughman or the child of a king, it is at the perfection of his manhood that we should aim. We are to be made men first, and ploughmen, merchants, manufacturers, artisans, authors, teachers, barristers, priests, or kings afterwards. We must teach first nobility of life ; we must teach character ; we must teach the love of honest, thorough work and its dignity ; we must teach the love of knowledge ; we must teach the enjoyment of what is simple, innocent, beautiful, and noble ; we must teach that sober reasonableness, that knowledge of the art of life, that wisdom by which alone we can guide our little bark in safety down the rapid brawling stream of life. And to teach all these good things we must first learn them.

[1] " What good, what ill hath in thine house befallen ' (Johnson's " Works," vii. 76).

" But Cristes lore, and his apostles twelve
He taught, but first he followed it himself."

The pettiness, the coarseness, the meanness, the
selfishness, the brutality of life meet us on all
sides.

" Shades of the prison-house begin to close
Upon the growing boy."

As we grow older cares and trouble come upon
us ; hopes are baffled, affections are wounded ;
death, who has silently watched our plan of life,
the pleasant habitation which we are slowly raising,
with a sudden rush sweeps one-half of it away ;
disease attacks us, and "Melancholy's phantoms
haunt our shade." We may have, too, our times
of prosperity, when all goes well with us. In our
youth we may gain prizes and exhibitions, scholar-
ships and fellowships ; we may thrive in business,
and grow in wealth ; we may be distinguished
schoolmasters, eminent physicians, leading queen's
counsel, great members of parliament, famous
divines ; we may have swum "this many summers
in a sea of glory," and the bladders on which we
float may never yet have burst. In all these
shifting scenes of life how is the balance of the
mind to be kept? The answer was given long
ages ago. "Wisdom is the principal thing, there-

fore get wisdom, and with all thy getting get
understanding."

No one, not even the outcast, not even the
poorest workhouse boy is to be trained as a mere
producing machine. He is to be made a man first
and a producer afterwards. "Misery," said Carlyle,
in describing his father's hard childhood, "misery
was early training the rugged boy into a stoic
that one day he might be the assurance of a
Scottish man." But misery is a hard and most
uncertain mistress. For the most part the children
trained by her sink to a lower level than the brutes.
It was not misery alone which trained James
Carlyle. He trusted besides, to use his son's
words, "to the scanty precepts of his mother, and
to what seeds or influences of culture were hanging,
as it were, in the atmosphere of his environment." [1]
Happy the household, however poor, where these
seeds, these influences are found ! Happy the
children who, in the talk round the family table,
hear tell of " golden days, fruitful in golden deeds ! "
Happy, too, are those whose "imagination is
stretched" while they are young, ere

> " Custom lie upon them with a weight,
> Heavy as frost, and deep almost as life."

---

[1] Carlyle's " Reminiscences," i. 36–7.

Look at the childhood of the greatest of Scottish peasants—Robert Burns. He was brought up in the hard school of poverty "with the unceasing moil," as he describes it, "of a galley-slave." But his father had struggled "to keep him and his other children under his own eye till they could discern between good and evil. He understood men, their manners, and their ways," and what he had learnt he taught his children. But the boy had another teacher, an old woman who resided in the family, "remarkable," Burns says, "for her ignorance, credulity, and superstition"; but I will venture to maintain a better infant schoolmistress for a young poet than any training-school could turn out. "She had the largest collection in the country of tales and songs concerning devils, ghosts, fairies, brownies, witches, warlocks, spunkies, kelpies, elf-candles, dead-lights, wraiths, apparitions, cantraips, giants, enchanted towers, dragons, and other trumpery. This," Burns continues, "cultivated the latent seeds of poetry." Old Northcote the painter, who in his boyhood had touched the skirt of Sir Joshua Reynolds's coat, who had known Goldsmith, and who lived to be asked by a little child named John Ruskin why there were holes in his carpet—Northcote, I say, talking one day to Hazlitt said : " ' Jack the Giant

Killer' is the first book I ever read, and I cannot describe the pleasure it gives me even now. I cannot look into it without my eyes filling with tears. I do not know what it is, whether good or bad, but it is to me, from early impressions, the most heroic of performances. I remember once not having money to buy it, and I transcribed it all out with my own hand. Had I been bred a scholar," he continues, "I dare say Homer would have been my Jack the Giant Killer." Charles Lamb, lamenting to Coleridge the banishment "of all the old classics of the nursery," says: "Think what you would have been now, if instead of being fed with tales and old wives' fables in childhood, you had been crammed with geography and natural history." It was not only with old wives' fables that Burns had been fed. By the village schoolmaster he was taught English, and taught it well. "The earliest composition," he says, "that I recollect taking pleasure in was 'The Vision of Mirza,' and a hymn of Addison's, beginning, 'How are Thy servants blest, O Lord!' I particularly remember one half stanza, which was music to my boyish ears:

> ' For though on dreadful whirls we hung
> High on the broken wave.'

I met with these pieces in Mason's 'English Collection,' one of my school-books. The two first books I ever read in private, and which gave me more pleasure than any two books I ever read since, were 'The Life of Hannibal' and 'The History of Sir William Wallace.' Hannibal gave my young ideas such a turn that I used to strut in raptures up and down after the recruiting-drum and bagpipe, and wish myself tall enough to be a soldier ; while the story of Wallace poured a Scottish prejudice into my veins, which will boil along there till the flood-gates of life shut in eternal rest." [1]

The flood-gates of life were not shut till the poet, with the old story still working in him, on the field of Bannockburn wrote his hymn of liberty.

There is no quality which more needs cultivating at the present day than imagination. It is killed by our civilization, it dies in the meanness of our great towns—in that " endless addition of littleness to littleness" to use Edmund Burke's description of London.[2] Not but that there are quarters in our great city where it may still be nourished. In the roar of its streets ; the hurrying to and fro of

[1] Burns's "Poems," ed. 1846, p. 15 ; "Conversations of Northcote," ed. 1830, p. 96 ; " Letters of Charles Lamb," ed. by A. Ainger, i. 189.
[2] " Correspondence of Edmund Burke," iii. 422.

eager multitudes; the gathering together of
travelled men from almost all the countries of the
world; the strange assemblage of commodities
where the East meets the West, and the North the
South; in the quiet courts and ancient buildings
lying so close to "the way of common trade," but
not of it; "the sky-like dome" of the great
cathedral; Westminster Abbey with its tombs of
"kings and counsellors of the earth," and its
Poets' Corner, where sleep men greater than kings
and counsellors; the Tower of London with its
little chapel "where the prisoners rest together";
Smithfield with its memory of the martyrs—in all
these we find abundant food for the imagination.
In spite of the vast growth of the unwieldly city,
and the ever-deepening gloom of its canopy of
smoke, now and then early in a summer morning,
or on a Sunday when ten thousand furnaces are
extinct, when the freshening wind or a passing
shower has cleared the air, we can still, as the
Thames flows beneath us, partake of the deep
feeling which moved Wordsworth, when eighty-
eight years ago standing on Westminster Bridge,
he composed his noble sonnet:

> "Earth has not anything to show more fair;
> Dull would he be of soul who could pass by
> A sight so touching in its majesty

This city now doth like a garment wear
The beauty of the morning ; silent, bare,
Ships, towers, domes, theatres, and temples lie
Open unto the fields, and to the sky ;
All bright and glittering in the smokeless air
Never did sun more beautifully steep
In his first splendour valley, rock, or hill ;
Ne'er saw I, never felt, a calm so deep !
The river glideth at his own sweet will :
Dear God ! the very houses seem asleep ;
And all that mighty heart is lying still ! "

To have such thoughts as these set stirring in us, it must be with a mind not unstored with knowledge that we wander through the streets. "He who would bring home the wealth of the Indies must carry the wealth of the Indies with him." But whatever impulses can be given to the imagination by the full and varied life of old London, how miserably is it starved by "the long unlovely streets" of the western quarter, and by the meanness of the poorer suburbs! I not unfrequently have to make my way from Holborn to Hampstead. On Staple Inn, with its fine old gables and its memories of Samuel Johnson, I cast "one longing, lingering look behind," and plunge into three or four miles of dejection. The eye droops and the spirit with it at the sight of prolonged and unmixed meanness. For a moment they may revive a little as I pass a large church-yard where flowers and trees have been lately planted, and walks thrown open, where the young play and the old rest ; they may even revive at the great Midland Railway Station at St. Pancras, for there man has aimed at magnificence ; but Camden Town, "that dismal world," beats them down lower than ever. They sink to rise no more. Few sadder thoughts come into my mind than when from the roof of the tramcar I look down upon street after street of children brought up in' the midst of this ugly meanness, with their imagination hopelessly starved. They may be happy enough under their smoky sky : they may "shout 'neath their sulphurous canopy " ; but it is the happiness of stunted growth, the shout far too often of coarse joy. One of the noblest qualities of the mind has in them received no nutriment. It is starved more-over by the advance of science, that is rapidly dispelling those clouds of superstition which, irra-diated by fancy, often cast a glow of beauty on every-day life.

" They fade into the light of common day."

It is with deep thankfulness that I see these clouds scattered, for they brought with them not

only beauty, but gloom and terror and cruelty.
But while we acknowledge the gain, let us not
shut our eyes to the loss. It was of this loss which
Lamb was thinking when he mourned over "the
old classics of the nursery." It was this loss
which moved Wordsworth so deeply when he
cried out:

> " The world is too much with us ; late and soon,
>   Getting and spending, we lay waste our powers:
>   Little we see in Nature that is ours ;
>   We have given our hearts away, a sordid boon !
>   This Sea that bares her bosom to the moon ;
>   The winds that will be howling at all hours,
>   And are up-gathered now like sleeping flowers ;
>   For this, for everything, we are out of tune ;
>   It moves us not. Great God ! I'd rather be
>   A Pagan suckled in a creed outworn ;
>   So might I, standing on this pleasant lea,
>   Have glimpses that would make me less forlorn ;
>   Have sight of Proteus rising from the sea ;
>   Or hear old Triton blow his wreathed horn."

Happy as Greece was in her mountains, and her
valleys, her clear sky and her deep blue sea with
its countless inlets and islands, still happier, I have
often thought, was she in her Homer. In the Iliad
and Odyssey she had two great poems which could
equally delight the child and solace the aged man.
No one was too young for them, no one too old.
The same splendid luminary which in every man

ushered in the dawn of thought and fancy, gave
light to his matured understanding, and with its
radiance did not desert his declining years. By
Homer's verse the ear of the child, while yet his
mind caught but little of its meaning, was trained
in the beauty of words and of rhythm ; by the
strange stories his imagination was stretched and
his eager curiosity awakened. By the praise of
great men and noble deeds his love of virtue and
of his country was roused. Much he could not at
first follow, but his little thoughts would be set
working. There was no writing down to his
understanding. He would struggle to rise to the
poet's level ; no bard of poems in words of one
syllable was required to come down to his. Single
lines, and then whole passages would fix themselves in his memory, where they would remain as
long as memory itself remained. They would
come back to him in the time of trial, in the Bay
of Salamis, and on the Plain of Marathon. They
would clothe the world in a vesture of beauty; they
would provide him with a refuge from the squalor
and meanness of his own surroundings; they would
give him a deep sense of the dignity of man ; they
would inspire him with a pride in his city. That
place, he was resolved, should be no mean city of
which he was a citizen. "Our poorest citizens,"

said Pericles, "have a keen relish for fine poetry, eloquence, art and grace of every kind." This, added Grote, "is what was true of Athens, and has never perhaps been true of any community since." It was mainly by Homer—Homer who accompanied the Athenian citizen from his cradle to his grave, that this relish was given. How deeply their great national poet moved the Greeks we can in some measure judge by the way in which it moves even us, who are strangers to their land, and parted from them by a wide waste of years. "I walked far into Herefordshire," writes Macaulay on a certain day in August, 1851, "and read, while walking, the last five books of the Iliad, with deep interest and many tears. I was afraid to be seen crying by the parties of walkers that met me as I came back : crying for Achilles cutting off his hair; crying for Priam rolling on the ground in the courtyard of his house ; mere imaginary beings, creatures of an old ballad-maker who died near three thousand years ago." [1]

Our English Bible, while it does much for us that Homer could never do, might have done far more for the imagination had it not been " soiled by all ignoble use." It is as noble a piece of prose

---

[1] "Life of George Grote," p. 203 ; "Life of Lord Macaulay," ed. 1877, ii. 297.

as any tongue can boast of; in its language it
stands side by side with Shakespeare. They are
the great twin brethren of English literature. But
on it have been hung system after system, creed
after creed. It has been used as the battle-field of
bigotry and dulness; as the torture chamber of
childhood ; as a dark hole in which imagination
and fancy, gaiety and all the joys of living should
be stifled. It has been turned into a task-book,
a book of impositions and punishments. It has
been treated as no other great work has ever
before been treated. Its most beautiful verses
have been stretched and expanded and paraphrased
till they cover more roods of print than Milton's
Satan covered of the burning flood. "Jesus wept"
was turned by the Rev. Dr. Harwood in his
"Liberal Translation of the New Testament" into
"the Saviour of the world burst into a flood of
tears." "Puppy," exclaimed Dr. Johnson, as he
contemptuously threw the book aside. But in the
church or chapel the child or youth cannot cry out
"Puppy!" when for three-quarters of an hour some
dull fellow turns a noble and beautiful thought into
a dreary wilderness of words. If he did he would
be caned by the beadle or indicted for brawling.
Then, too, there are those who, with what Addison
calls "a natural uncheerfulness of heart, are scan-

dalized at youth for being lively, and at childhood
for being playful. They sit at a christening
or a marriage-feast as at a funeral, sigh at
the conclusion of a merry story, and grow devout
when the rest of the company grow pleasant."[1] In
the hands of such people as these the Scriptures
are only used as a rude weapon of offence, as a
stick to beat a sinner with. In after days by that
strange association of ideas which plays such freaks
with us, it only too commonly happens that the
sight of the Bible, after this cruel misuse of it, at
once rouses in the mind a feeling of dulness and
depression. To many, I gladly own, it always remains the freshest of books. It fed John Bunyan,
a man unsurpassed in imagination. From it John
Milton drew one-half of his inspiration, and John
Bright the best part of his noble oratory. Even
with all its misuse it is the book which most of all
has carried imagination into children's hearts. It
might in all of us remain throughout life the chief
source of that sublime faculty were it not degraded
from its high post by man's dulness. In these
latter days a worse evil than ever has befallen it ;
it has got into the stifling grasp of school-inspec-

---

[1] Boswell's "Life of Johnson," iii. 39 ; *The Spectator*,
No. 494.

tors and examiners.   Against them "even the Gods strive in vain."

In the dulness of modern life imagination is still further starved.   Of old in the stately processions of the court, of the church, and of the guilds a rich and varied colouring was given to our streets. The signboards over the shops, with their pictures of more animals than are known to nature, and the bright colours of the clothes commonly worn, lent life and animation to the scene.   Even the men of last century, scorned as they are for their want of fancy, wore coats of blue and green and scarlet.   Goldsmith's bloom-coloured coat must have helped to brighten Fleet Street.   The Goddess of Dulness had not yet appeared under her new name of Respectability, with her worshippers wearing black coats and tall silk hats.

> " Before her fancy's gilded clouds decay,
>   And all its varying rainbows die away."

Even Oxford has turned traitor.   The gown which gave so picturesque a look to her streets is now but little worn, and is likely before very long to become a relic of the past.   Men are afraid of being suspected of taking pride in wearing it. Strangers in the coming century will be heard saying, with the change of but one word in Tennyson's lines :

" I past beside the reverend walls
In which of old *they* wore the gown."

Even in our very playgrounds imagination is struck with decay. It was said by Dr. Arbuthnot, that "most universal genius" of Queen Anne's days, "that nowhere is tradition preserved pure and incorrupt but among schoolboys, whose games and plays are handed down invariably the same from one generation to another." [1] A single generation has, however, seen more games die out than it took fifty generations to invent. They may, perhaps, linger in the smaller schools in out-of-the-way places, but they are everywhere, I fear, fast disappearing. Lads play solemnly and by system. They take their games as their forefathers were said to take their pleasures—sadly. We no longer see

" Four-and-twenty happy boys
Come bounding out of school."

They first put on their flannels, and then stride forth majestically. The delightful naturalness of games, the unbounded freedom, the perfect simplicity in which all was forgotten but the joy of playing is known no more. Jack runs and jumps, not because

[1] Swift's "Works," ed. 1803, xxiii. 22.

11

" He lightly draws his breath,
And feels his life in every limb ; "

but that he may run a hundred yards in a quarter
of a second less than Harry, or jump an eighth of
an inch higher than Tom. A cricket match is
carried on with a gravity which would not disgrace
a set of undertakers. Every part of it is afterwards dissected as minutely as the anatomist
dissects a muscle, and analyzed as carefully as a
new substance in chemistry. Averages are struck
and results are published with far greater accuracy
than we can hope ever to see attained in the census
paper. Football is put under law-givers almost as
severe as Draco, and is managed by marshals who
at every moment are throwing their warders down.
Many a game which delighted my boyhood—as,
no doubt, it had delighted the boyhood of
countless generations—is no longer played. For
every five games I knew, my sons, I verily believe,
when they were at school, scarce knew one. When
the modern Etonian reads—perhaps I should say
if he reads—Gray's " Distant Prospect of Eton
College," with what a smile of disdain must he
learn " that his predecessors " chased the rolling
circle's speed " : in other words, bowled a hoop.
Low as Eton once was, Harrow was almost lower.
One hundred and thirty years ago, two boys, after-

wards famous as great scholars—Sir William Jones
and Dr. Parr—" divided the fields in the neighbourhood of the school, according to a map of
Greece, into states and kingdoms ; each fixed upon
one as his dominion, and assumed an ancient
name. Some of their schoolfellows consented to
be styled barbarians, who were to invade their ter-
ritories and attack their hillocks, which were
denominated fortresses. The chiefs vigorously
defended their respective domains against the
incursions of the enemy : and in these imitative
wars the young statesmen held councils, made
vehement harangues, and composed memorials—
all doubtless very boyish, but calculated to fill
their minds with ideas of legislation and civil
government." So wrote Sir William Jones's
biographer, Lord Teignmouth, a man who holds
a high post among the legislators and governors
of India.

Just as young Jones had turned the fields of
Harrow into Grecian states, so a few years later,
in the north of Scotland, James Mackintosh, who,
like Jones, was destined to become known as an
Indian judge and famous as a scholar, turned his
school into the Roman Empire. " Before I was
fourteen," he writes, " I read the old translation of
Plutarch's 'Lives' and Echard's 'Roman His-

tory.' I well remember that the perusal of the last led me into a ridiculous habit, from which I shall never be totally free. I used to fancy myself Emperor of Constantinople; I distributed offices and provinces amongst my schoolfellows. I loaded my favourites with dignity and power, and I often made the object of my dislike feel the weight of my imperial resentment. I carried on the series of political events in solitude for several hours; I resumed them and continued them from day to day for months." [1]

Games such as these, if they did not swell to the full the calves of the legs and the muscles of the arms, at all events fed the imagination. I look back with delight to the sports of my childhood, free and full of variety, changing sometimes with the seasons, but more often with our caprices, unvexed by training and competition, and untainted by publicity and prizes. As I charged at a rough game called "hoppy," I used to think myself the Black Knight or Ivanhoe; as I stole through the trees at hide-and-seek, I was the Last of the Mohicans or Deerslayer. How delightful was the paper-chase in the forest, as the hares led us we knew not where, from thicket to thicket and

[1] "Life of Sir William Jones," p. 25 ; "Life of Sir James Mackintosh," i. 5.

from glade to glade! At the present time in the great schools, I am told, the course they shall take is all laid down beforehand. It is along roads, not through woods and fields, that they are to run, and glory, not joy, is the reward of the chase. Watch in hand, the umpire awaits their return, who, with the accuracy of an astronomer and the gravity of a judge, records the exact number of minutes and seconds each has taken, and then prepares his report for the next number of the *School Magazine*, or even of some sporting newspaper.

Formality and dulness, which had long been contented with their empire over religion and learning have indeed with rapid advance extended their sway over our playing-fields. They have gathered under it not only those who do play, but also those who do not. A football match is going on : fifteen youths on either side are rapidly covering themselves with mud and glory ; but however plentiful may be the mud, their glory cannot be complete without a large ring of spectators. The whole school must be swept together to stand round and applaud. The boy who loves the fields and nature, solitude and meditation, and who wanders away,

"Step following step, and thought by thought led on,"

is reproached not only by his playmates, but by his dull masters with his want of " patriotism.' " Patriotism " Johnson defined as " the last refuge of a scoundrel " ; had he lived now he would have been indignant at the base use to which it can be put by a blockhead.   Let us hope that, in defiance of the law of public opinion, not less strong because it is unwritten, and in spite of the reproaches cast upon them, in scorn of the strong man's contumely,

> " Some bold adventurers disdain
>   The limits of their little reign,
>   And unknown regions dare descry :
>   Still as they run they look behind,
>   They hear a voice in every wind,
>   And snatch a fearful joy."

One such adventurer, a poet ever dear to him to whom Nature is dear, thus describes his schoolboy rambles :

> " For I have loved the rural walk through lanes
>   Of grassy swarth, close-cropt by nibbling sheep,
>   And skirted thick with intertexture firm
>   Of thorny boughs : have loved the rural walk
>   O'er hills, through valleys, and by river's brink,
>   E'er since a truant boy I passed my bounds
>   T' enjoy a ramble on the banks of Thames.
>   And still remember, nor without regret
>   Of hours that sorrow since has much endear'd,
>   How oft, my slice of pocket store consumed,

Still hung'ring, pennyless, and far from home,
I fed on scarlet hips and stony haws,
Or blushing crabs, or berries that imboss
The bramble, black as jet, or sloes austere."

It was not with the ramble that the enjoyment ceased. It remained with Cowper through the long years of his troubled life.

" Youth repairs
His wasted spirits quickly, by long toil
Incurring short fatigue ; and though our years,
As life declines, speed rapidly away,
And not a year but pilfers as he goes
Some youthful grace that age would gladly keep,
A tooth or auburn lock, and by degrees
Their length and colour from the locks they spare ;
Th' elastic spring of an unwearied foot
That mounts the stile with ease, or leaps the fence,
That play of lungs inhaling and again
Respiring freely the fresh air, that makes
Swift pace or steep ascent no toil to me,
Mine have not pilfer'd yet ; nor yet impair'd
My relish of fair prospect ; scenes that sooth'd
Or charmed me young, no longer young, I find
Still soothing and of power to charm me still."

If modern patriotism came to an end with schooldays, though the mischief done would still be vast, a partial cure might yet be found. But this patriotic habit, once formed, follows our youths from the school to the university. In the autumn

term, two or three times every week, a dense ring
is formed in the Parks round the football-ground.
On some bright day early in November, when the
beauty of the late autumn calls us forth with a
summons that cannot be withstood, not only
because the beauty is so great, but because we
know that its life is so brief, a thousand of these
patriots are massed together. What care they
that the wind is blowing fresh on Cumner Hurst
or on Shotover? what care they that "the flying
gold of the ruined woodland drives through the
air"? Their duty requires them for the space of
one hour to bawl out in their vile slang, "Well
played 'Varsity!" They know nothing of country
rambles, the delight of country walks. If a friend
tries to tempt them abroad, they sternly push him
aside, as Regulus pushed aside his kinsmen and the
crowd who would delay his return to Carthage and
to death. I once met in Switzerland two Oxo-
nians, fine young fellows and great athletes, but as
ignorant as a child in long clothes of the art of
walking. Apparently they had not so much as
heard that there was a country round about
Oxford. Their outdoor life, both here and at
school, had been all spent in the cricket-field or
the football-ground. With the son of Alcinous,
they would have said:

" Οὐ μὲν γὰρ μεῖζον κλέος ἀνέρος, ὄφρα κεν, ᾖσιν,
ἢ ὅτι ποσσίν τε 'ρέξει καὶ χερσὶν ἐῇσιν."

" For greater praise
Hath no man while he lives, than that he know
His feet to exercise and hands aright."

How far otherwise had Thysis sought his strength,
that refined and gentle poet whom his brother
bard, now himself taken from us, so gracefully
lamented :

" And this rude Cumner ground,
    Its fir-topped Hurst, its farms, its quiet fields,
    Here cam'st thou in thy jocund youthful time,
    Here was thine height of strength, thy golden prime !
    And still the haunt beloved a virtue yields."

A man of my time of life must mourn with Cowper
over many things that the years have taken from
him, but over one thing he may rejoice. He was
born when games were still thoughtless and free.

" Ere the base laws of servitude began,
    When wild in woods the *happy schoolboy* ran."

Happy, too, were we that we had to seek our
heroes elsewhere than in the columns of sporting
newspapers. In those simple days there was, I
believe, but one paper of that dull class published
in the whole of England. It came forth but once
a week and cost sixpence. No names of mighty

cricketers, football players, jumpers and runners were familiar in our mouths. I cannot call to mind that even in my undergraduate days their fame troubled us. In our eager talk we travelled far and wide, but on athletics we never touched. In the university "sports," as they are called, were unknown, and, so far as my memory serves, so also were football matches. At all events, if they went on, they were not conspicuous. Even the Oxford and Cambridge cricket match at Lord's was watched by few. He who strolled in to see it sauntered where he wished, or lay at full length on the grass with no one to obstruct the view.

Had Themistocles lived now-a-days it would not have been the trophies of Miltiades which would not suffer him to sleep, but the live ox carried by Milo over the race-course of Olympia. Had he come up to Oxford, it would not have been "o'er Bodley's Dome," but over the Parks that his future labours would have spread. In my first lecture I read to you the fine passage in which Johnson describes a scholar's career. I will now venture to read a parody on it which I published last year in the *Speaker*:

> " When first the College rolls receive their names
> The young enthusiasts quit their work for games :
> Through all their limbs the fever of renown

Leads them to scorn the labours of the gown :
O'er football fields their future labours spread,
And many a foe they tumble on his head.
Are these your views ? Proceed illustrious souls
And hacking bring you to the football goals.
Yet, should your limbs succeed in every heat
Till all your records there is none to beat ;
Should training guide you in the wisest way
And send you perfect to the racing day ;
Should no false kindness lure to drink all night,
No pipes relax, nor early risings fright ;
Should tempting pastrycooks your rooms refrain,
And sloth effuse Virginian fumes in vain ;
Should beauty blunt on dons her fatal dart,
Nor claim to triumph o'er the trainer's art ;
Should no disease spoil ' Torpids' or the ' Eights,'
Or melancholy thoughts of coming ' Greats ' ;
Yet hope not life from schools or cramming free,
Nor think the doom of pluck reversed for ye.
Deign on the passman's world to turn your eyes,
And pause awhile from kicking to be wise.
There mark what ills the athlete's life attack,
Sprains, bruises, bumps, at times a broken back.
See Guardians, wisely slow and meanly just
To worn-out athletes throw the workhouse crust ;
If ' Blues ' yet flatter, once again attend,
Or else in looking blue your life will end."

It is a melancholy change when in the columns
of sporting papers not in the pages of poetry,
romance and history ; in the record of "events,"
as they are absurdly called, not in Froissart,
Shakespeare, Defoe, and Scott, that our heroes are
sought for and found. " Teach us to admire," the

Master of Balliol is reported to have said to a newly-appointed Professor of Poetry. It is a lesson that should not have to be taught in such a spot as this. If he were to keep silence the very stones would cry out. Listen to the words which one of the great band of poets who are the peculiar glory of Cambridge wrote of his famous College :

> " I could not print
> Ground where the grass had yielded to the steps
> Of generations of illustrious men,
> Unmoved. I could not always lightly pass
> Through the same gateways, sleep where they had slept,
> Wake where they waked, range that enclosure old,
> That garden of great intellects, undisturbed."

LECTURE VI.

LECTURE VI.

THE feelings which would naturally rise in us on hearing of great men and great deeds may be stifled in our youth. Chill pedantry quite as much as chill penury may—

> " repress the noble rage
> And freeze the genial current of the soul."

"What would you give my lad," said Johnson to a boy who was sculling him and Boswell on the Thames, "what would you give to know about the Argonauts?" "Sir," said the boy, "I would give what I have." Johnson turning to Boswell, "sir," said he, "a desire of knowledge is the natural feeling of mankind; and every human being, whose mind is not debauched, will be willing to give all that he has to get knowledge." There are many things which may debauch the mind. It may be debauched by competition and cramming.

The love of knowledge cannot be planted by examiners or watered by inspectors. It is not they who can give the increase. I am not so foolish as to deny that examiners and inspectors have their use. A needful, nay a great part, of teaching consists in implanting habits of accuracy and in giving the power of mastering subjects which are difficult and sometimes dry and distasteful. "It is no doubt," wrote John Mill, "a very laudable effort in modern teaching to render as much as possible of what the young are required to learn easy and interesting to them. But when this principle is pushed to the length of not requiring them to learn anything but what has been made easy and interesting, one of the chief objects of education is sacrificed. I rejoice in the decline of the old brutal and tyrannical system of teaching, which, however, did succeed in enforcing habits of application ; but the new, as it seems to me, is training up a race of men who will be incapable of doing anything which is disagreeable to them." [1]

I am as fully alive as any one to the evils of what he meant by the new system, for under it my own education greatly suffered. But while to

[1] Boswell's "Johnson," i. 458 ; "Autobiography of Mill," p. 52.

guard against these evils, and against indolent and inaccurate teaching also, we use examiners and inspectors, let us resist, as far as we can, their invasion of that part of the mind where they can only work havoc. " A cow is a very good animal in a field, but we turn her out of a garden." Examiners and school inspectors like cows are always trying to break in where by their clumsy trampling they can only do mischief. To keep them out needs a far stronger hedge than as yet has anywhere been provided. They encourage display—a great evil in every part and period of life, but doubly great in education. For it is most successfully made not by the good, but by the dexterous teacher ; not in the higher, but in the lower faculties of the mind. It is not the reasoning powers, not the powers of the fancy and imagination which are tested and exhibited. It is not the eager desire for knowledge, the teacher's crowning glory, that can be measured. He who has implanted that has done even more than the Sirens promised. Whoever comes to us, they sang, goes on his way full of delight and with increase of knowledge. But to delight and knowledge the good teacher adds a still greater gift—an ardent and noble curiosity, an eager desire to know more. " I will back Shenstone's

12

schoolmistress," says Wordsworth, " by her winter
fire and in her summer garden-seat against all Dr.
Bell's sour-looking teachers in petticoats that I
have seen." We can easily believe that, partly
because he looked on all things too much with the
eye of a solitary poet, and partly because as age
came on him he clung too much to the past, he
failed to see whatever there was of good in the
new system of education. Nevertheless, his admiration of Shenstone's Village Dame had some
justification. Her children would scarcely, perhaps,
have passed the lowest standard ; yet she may
have had one or two of the best qualities of the
teacher. History certainly has often been far
worse taught. The poet describes her garden and
continues :

" Here oft the dame, on Sabbath's decent eve,
  Hymned such psalms as Sternhold forth did mete ;
  If winter 'twere, she to her hearth did cleave ;
  But in her garden found a summer-seat :
  Sweet melody ! to hear her then repeat
  How Israel's sons, beneath a foreign king,
  While taunting foemen did a song entreat,
  All for the nonce untuning every string,
  Uphung their useless lyres—small heart had they to sing.

  For she was just, and friend to virtuous lore,
  And pass'd much time in truly virtuous deed ;
  And, in those elfins' ears, would oft deplore

The times when Truth by Popish rage did bleed,
And tortious death was true Devotion's meed ;
And simple Faith in iron chains did mourn,
That nould [1] on wooden image place her creed ;
And lawny saints in smouldering flames did burn ;
Ah! dearest Lord! forfend thilk days should e'er return."

Her history, if it was rude, was at all events a
living thing. It was no "old almanac," no mere
system of dull chronology and empty lifeless
names. It was the imagination, and not the
memory she exercised. England of the Reforma-
tion was to her a real and terrible, but very noble
thing, which must be pictured to her little scholars
so that when they grew up they might each to the
utmost strive against "the triple tyrant." She had
her learning, no doubt, fresh from Fox's "Book
of Martyrs" and "The Pilgrim's Progress."
School histories, those instruments of torture,
had not yet been invented. They are like the
dungeon in the Tower of London called Little
Ease, where the unhappy prisoner could not stand,
sit, or lie in any comfort. They cramp the understanding, they choke the imagination. They are
worse than no food at all, for they take away
appetite and they afford no nourishment. Happily
for me when I was young, Goldsmith—unabridged

[1] *Nould* is *would not.*

Goldsmith—had not been banished from the schoolroom, and in his delightful pages Greece and Rome had a real life. Into errors enough he fell no doubt, for accuracy was not his strongest point. In his "Animated Nature" he makes the cow shed her horns every year. But he did not fall into dulness. His Greeks and Romans lived for us ; I loved the just Aristides and the mild Camillus. They were as real to me as Robinson Crusoe and Friday. No place on earth was dearer to me than the little town of Platæa. Its sad and glorious story as told in Dr. Smith's "School History" could not ruffle the surface of the mind for a single moment, or remain in it, unless supported by the hope of rewards or the fear of punishment, for a single week. But I read it in the pages of Goldsmith, that

" Affectuum potens at lenis dominator ; "

that gentle master of passion, who—

" sways it to the mood
Of what he likes or loathes,"

and having there read it, I am still inspired, after the lapse of six and forty years, with a love of the

little town, and a longing to visit the spot where
it once stood.

What a difference, too, do we find in the story
of the ostracism of Aristides as narrated by the
man of industry and the man of genius! "We
are told," writes Dr. Smith, "that an unlettered
countryman gave his vote against Aristides, at the
ostracism, because he was tired of hearing him
always called the ' Just.' " Here we certainly have
all that we need have to enable us to appear with
confidence before an examiner. *Question.* "Why
did a countryman vote against Aristides ? "
Answer. "Because he was tired of hearing him
always called the Just." Result—a good mark
scored down by the examiner, and the story in
a few days forgotten by the boy. Now listen
to Goldsmith's story :—" It was on this occasion
that a peasant who could not write, and did not
know Aristides personally, applied to him himself
and desired him to write the name of Aristides
upon the shell by which his vote was given against
him. 'Has he done you any wrong?' said
Aristides, 'that you are for condemning him in
this manner?' 'No,' replied the peasant, 'but
I hate to hear him praised for his justice.'
Aristides, without saying a word more, calmly
took the shell. wrote down his name upon it,

and contentedly retired into banishment." That
is a story that might surely stir a child's heart,
and inspire him with a generous sentiment which
should last his life through. Goldsmith, if he tells
a thing at all, tells it fully and well. He was not
cramped by the need of getting into his narrative
everything on which a question could by any
possibility be founded. If an incident could move
the mind he dwelt on it; if it was uninteresting
in itself he passed it over.

Happy as the Greeks were in their poet, scarcely
less happy were they in their historian. Herodotus,
like Homer, could delight childhood and old age
alike. There is nothing in his pages which the
schoolboy would have skipped because he could
not understand it, or the old man because it was
childish. It delights us still.

> " Age cannot wither it, nor custom stale
> Its infinite variety."

Though we have no Homer or Herodotus,
nevertheless we can still to a large extent keep
our children in the company of great writers.
In poetry, in fiction, in history, in biography, I
would almost add in geography, I would have
none read but great authors—authors whom we
should love the more in our old age because they

had been the delight of our youth. Through the whole of English history we could not take a boy in the narrative of one great writer as a young Athenian could have been taken in the narrative of Herodotus ; nevertheless, by means of selections, we could keep him almost always among big men. It would matter little that there were gaps in his knowledge ; there are great gaps in every one's knowledge, even in the knowledge of examiners. If we have succeeded in making the past really live for the child in a single century, nay, I will say in a single year ; if we have made him feel that, "in the dark backward and abysm of time," men "lived and moved and had their being," our teaching has not been in vain. I remember talking to a countryman at Old Sarum, where a huge mound marks the site of an ancient town. He told me that some graves had lately been found there of men who had fallen in a great battle. " But that was afore my time," he added, by way of apology for his want of accurate information. I remember likewise telling another countryman of the war which had just broken out between France and Germany. " I hope it won't do my brother any harm," he said. "Your brother," I replied, " How should he be harmed ? " " Why, he has lately gone to America," was the answer. To the rude mind there are but

two times and two places—"my time," and what
was "afore my time"; "my village," and the rest
rest of the world.   Both these countrymen had, I
daresay, attended school; one of them certainly
had.   But what notion can be formed of the wide
world by mere maps and barren books of geography,
or what of the succession of time by tables of
chronology and bald statements of events?   What
knowledge of the past has the child got, though he
knows perfectly the succession of the Kings of
Israel, and can tell without a moment's hesitation
that Pekah succeeded Pekahiah and not Pekahiah
Pekah?   "What is Hecuba to him or he to
Hecuba?"   If all these kings are anything more
to him than mere names, they are all "afore his
time," and all no farther or nearer off than the
kings of England.   It is by imagination alone
that we throw a bridge across time and space.   If
imagination is not made the foundation and the
buttress, their labour is but lost that build it.   It
is a quality inherent in all but the lowest natures,
though far too often it is never developed.   Often,
too, though fanned into life in the nursery by
stories of fairies and giants, it is deadened in the
parlour by dulness and respectability, and finally
destroyed in the schoolroom by school-books and
bad teaching.   It may be destroyed even by great

writers if they are either forced upon us at an age
when we are unfit for them, or if they are misused
as instruments of teaching. A friend of mine in
this University told me that before he had come
up to Oxford he had read the "Æneid" through
with great delight. Here, in preparing for the
examination known as Moderations, he was taken
through it by his tutor once more, who treated
Virgil not as a great poet, but as a convenient
instrument of instruction in the niceties of grammar.
Under the guidance of this teacher—

> " One whose hand,
> Like the base Indian, threw a pearl away,
> Richer than all his tribe "—

my friend gained his first class and lost for ever his
enjoyment of the " Æneid."

The man who would use a great poet for
beating grammar into a boy, who would parse
" Hamlet " and analyze the " Paradise Lost,"
would not for one moment hesitate to

> " botanize
> Upon his mother's grave."

The proper destination for bad poets should not
be the shop,

> " Where pepper, odours, frankincense are sold,
> And all small wares in wretched rhymes enrolled,"

but the school grammar. Cobbett went to King's Speeches for his examples of bad English. *Experimentum fiat in corpore vili.* If you must teach grammatical analysis get it out of Tupper. Remember how the Ensign in " Tom Jones " damned Homer with all his heart, saying that he carried the marks of him on his back. When, in still coarser language, he goes on to reproach Corderius's mother with want of virtue, we listen to his abuse with more patience. For between Corderius and Homer there is almost as much difference as between Lindley Murray and Shakespeare.

Happy is the child who has the run of a good library, and who for a certain part of every day is allowed to read at random ; who is turned loose in the rich pasture of English literature to browse where he pleases! It would be a wise practice in every school, with as much regularity as the morning prayer comes round, to read aloud some fine or interesting passage from a book which was accessible to him who wished to read more. A friend of mine took into her house a poor child who had fallen sick in one of the London board schools. Seeing " Ivanhoe " on the shelf, he asked for leave to read it. Having in some book of extracts read the storming of Front-de-Boeuf's castle, he longed to know the rest of the story. It is not needful that every word of what is read aloud should be understood by the hearers. If that were the case, the Epistles of St. Paul would be a sealed book to all but scholars. Sir Walter Scott, in his too brief "Autobiography," writing of an old friend of his father's who was the original of "Jonathan Oldbuck" in the *Antiquary*, says: "He was the first person who told me about Falstaff and Hotspur and other characters in Shakespeare. What idea I annexed to them I know not, but I must have annexed some, for I remember quite well being interested in the subject. Indeed, I rather suspect," he goes on to say, "that children derive impulses of a powerful kind in hearing things which they cannot entirely comprehend; and therefore that to write down to children's understanding is a mistake; set them on the scent and let them puzzle it out."[1] Something they can always grasp; and what they cannot understand they either supply by some strange meaning of their own, or else let it pass by unheeded. Let me illustrate this by a little anecdote. At the time of the Hungarian War of Independence my grandfather, whose sight was dimmed by eighty-six years, had the newspaper read aloud to him by a lad from the village school. One of his daughters,

[1] Lockhart's "Life of Scott," ed. 1839, i. 34.

coming one morning into his room, was astonished at hearing some such account of the campaign as the following: "Early in the morning General Jerusalem, breaking up his quarters, led his soldiers to Jerusalem, where they fell on Marshal Jerusalem's army, which they drove in headlong flight as far as Jerusalem, where they found an unexpected support in Colonel Jerusalem's cavalry." "Why, father," said his daughter, in amazement, "what strange stuff is this?" "Oh," replied the old gentleman, with a chuckle, "the boy could make nothing of the names of the Hungarians, Russians, and Austrians; so I said to him: 'Do as the dame-school mistress bade her scholars do when they came to a hard word in reading the Bible, "Say *Jerusalem*, my dears, and pass on."'" A child can say *Jerusalem* for himself without being told to, and will willingly go on saying it, provided that there is enough left that he can understand and enjoy. "He should not be discouraged from reading anything that he takes a liking to, from a notion that it is above his reach. If that be the case, he will soon find it out and and desist." [1] By wandering, as it were, among books, each one finds out where his strength and enjoyment most lie.

[1] Boswell's "Life of Johnson," iv. 21.

It is often at a very early age that the mind is influenced. Sir William Jones, we are told, was only in his fifth year, "when one morning, turning over the pages of a Bible in his mother's closet, his attention was forcibly arrested by the sublime description of the Angel in the tenth chapter of the Apocalyse; the impression which his imagination received from it was never effaced." [1]

Harriet Martineau, whose " Settlers at Home " and " Feats on the Fiord " I hope still give to children the pleasure which they gave to me, tells how, one winter Sunday afternoon, when she was seven years old, she was kept from chapel by some ailment. " When the house-door closed behind the chapel-goers," she continues, " I looked at the books on the table. The ugliest-looking of them was turned down open ; and my turning it up was one of the leading incidents of my life. That plain, clumsy, calf-bound volume was ' Paradise Lost,' and the common blueish paper, with its old-fashioned type, became as a scroll out of heaven to me. The first thing I saw was Argument, which I took to mean a dispute, and supposed to be stupid enough ; but there was something about Satan cleaving Chaos, which made me turn to the poetry ; and my mental destiny was fixed

[1] " Life of Sir William Jones," p. 17.

for the next seven years. That volume was henceforth never to be found but by asking me for it, till a young acquaintance made me a present of a little Milton of my own. In a few months, I believe there was hardly a line in ' Paradise Lost ' that I could not have instantly turned to. I sent myself to sleep by repeating it ; and when my curtains were drawn back in the morning, descriptions of heavenly light rushed into my memory." [1]

Shenstone, who had learnt to read of the old dame whom he has described in his " Schoolmistress," " soon received such delight from books, that he was always calling for fresh entertainment, and expected that, when any of the family went to market, a new book should be brought him, which, when it came, was in fondness carried to bed and laid by him. It is said that, when his request had been neglected, his mother wrapped up a piece of wood of the same form, and pacified him for the night." Sir Joshua Reynolds was but eight when he received his turn for painting by reading the " ' Jesuit's Perspective,' a book which happened to be in the parlour window in his

---

[1] " Autobiography of Harriet Martineau," i. 42. We have here an instance of that inaccuracy which too often marred Miss Martineau's work. There is nothing in the " Argument " about " Satan cleaving Chaos."

father's house." A blessing on the houses of old which were built with walls thick enough for window-seats, where people sat and read and left books about for children to dip into. It was in a window in his mother's room that Cowley, when a little child, found Spenser's " Fairy Queen," and so by reading it, "became, as he relates, irrecoverably a poet." [1]

Gibbon, when a boy of ten, was well acquainted with Pope's " Homer " and the " Arabian Nights." " The verses of Pope," he writes, " accustomed my ear to the sound of poetic harmony ; in the death of Hector and the shipwreck of Ulysses I tasted the new emotions of terror and pity ; and seriously disputed with my aunt on the vices and virtues of the heroes of the Trojan war." He had attended school for a short time, but his twelfth year he passed in his aunt's house where he had the command of a library. " I turned over," he continues, " many English pages of poetry and romance, of history and travels. Where a title attracted my eye, without fear or awe I snatched the volume from the shelf ; and my aunt, who indulged herself in moral and religious speculations, was more prone to encourage than to check a curiosity above the

[1] Johnson's " Works," vii. 1 ; viii. 408 ; Prior's " Life of Malone," p. 389.

strength of a boy. This year I shall note as the
most propitious to the growth of my intellectual
stature." The most learned of English historians,
when he looked back on his past life, considered,
you will observe, that his mind grew the fastest in
in a year when he was under no regular teacher,
but was left to " that free, desultory reading, which
was," he tells us, " the employment and comfort of
his solitary hours." [1]

Johnson had the great good fortune to have the
run of a bookseller's shop, for his father was in that
trade. When he was quite a child the old man put
into his little boy's hands Martin's " Account of the
Western Islands of Scotland." It was the longing
excited in him by that book to see the places
therein described, which nearly sixty years later,
more perhaps than anything else, led him to undertake his adventurous tour to the Hebrides. When
he was sixteen he left school. In the next two
years " he read a great deal in a desultory manner,
without any scheme of study, as chance threw
books in his way, and inclination directed him
through them. He used to mention one curious
instance of his casual reading, when but a boy.
Having imagined that his brother had hid some
apples behind a large folio upon an upper shelf in

[1] Gibbon's " Miscellaneous Works," i. 34, 40.

his father's shop, he climbed up to search for them. There were no apples; but the large folio proved to be ' Petrarch,' whom he had seen mentioned in some preface as one of the restorers of learning. His curiosity having been thus excited, he sat down with avidity, and read a great part of the book." It was no doubt the remembrance of this eager reading which made him say in his old age: "That for general improvement, a man should read whatever his immediate inclination prompts him to ; though to be sure, if a man has a science to learn, he must regularly and resolutely advance." He added, "What we read with inclination makes a much stronger impression. If we read without inclination half the mind is employed in fixing the attention; so there is but one half to be employed on what we read."[1] Tranio in " The Taming of the Shrew " had given much the same advice to his master, Lucentio :

> " No profit grows where is no pleasure ta'en ;
> In brief, sir, study what you most affect."

A few years after Johnson visited Scotland, Walter Scott was a little boy at the High School of Edinburgh. "In the intervals of my school hours," Scott writes, "I had always perused with

[1] Boswell's " Life of Johnson," i. 57, 450; iii. 43.

avidity such books of history or poetry or voyages
and travels as chance presented to me—not for-
getting the usual, or rather ten times the usual
quantity of fairy tales, eastern stories and romances. These studies were totally unregulated
and undirected. My tutor thought it almost a sin
to open a profane play or poem. I found in my
mother's dressing-room, where I slept at one time,
some odd volumes of 'Shakespeare,' nor can I
easily forget the rapture with which I sat up in
my shirt reading them by the light of a fire in her
apartment, until the bustle of the family rising
from supper warned me it was time to creep back
to my bed, where I was supposed to have been
safely deposited since nine o'clock." [1]

Wordsworth, writing of his life at Hawkshead
Grammar School, whither he was sent in his ninth
year, says: "Of my earliest days at school I have
little to say but that they were very happy ones,
chiefly because I was at liberty then and in the
vacations to read whatever books I liked. For
example, I read all Fielding's works, 'Don
Quixote,' 'Gil Blas,' and any part of Swift that
I liked; 'Gulliver's Travels,' and the 'Tale of a
Tub,' being both much to my taste." This desultory reading he carried on even at the University.

[1] Lockhart's " Life of Scott," i. 49.

" He did not tread," says his pompous biographer,
"in the beaten path, prescribed by academic
authority and leading to academic distinctions.
He appears to have indulged a feeling of intellectual pride in taking a devious course—much to
the disappointment of his relatives and friends.
His last summer vacation was not spent amid his
books, but among the Alps. The week before
he took his degree he passed his time in reading
'Clarissa Harlowe.'" It is possible that "academic authority" was wrong, and the young poet
was right. There are other "overseeing powers"
besides a University Senate, "to kindle or re-
strain." A Board of Examiners is not infallible;
that student may not do ill to whom, in contempt
of it, nature is "both law and impulse." There are
those whom Ferguson, "the self-taught philosopher," calls "God Almighty's scholars."[1] I knew
three undergraduates, contemporaries and friends
of my own in this University, who might be
reproached with "the same intellectual pride" as
Wordsworth, "in taking a devious course," who,
nevertheless, are not the least distinguished men
of their time—Mr. Burne-Jones, Mr. Morris, the

[1] "Life of William Wordsworth," ed. 1851, i. 10, 48 ;
James Ferguson's " Select Mechanical Exercises," ed. 1778,
p. xi.

author of the "Earthly Paradise," and Mr. Swinburne.

Charles Darwin, the greatest of naturalists, did so little in the seven or eight years he passed at Shrewsbury School, that his father one day, to his "deep mortification," said to him : "You care for nothing but shooting, dogs, and rat-catching, and you will be a disgrace to yourself and all your family." "Nothing," Darwin writes, "could have been worse for the development of my mind than Dr. Butler's school, as it was strictly classical, nothing else being taught except a little ancient geography and history. Looking back," he continues, "as well as I can at my character during my school life, the only qualities which at this period promised well for the future were that I had strong and diversified tastes, much zeal for whatever interested me, and a keen pleasure in understanding any complex subject or thing. . . . I was fond of reading various books, and I used to sit for hours reading the historical plays of Shakespeare in an old window in the thick walls of the school." Here we have the old window-seat once more doing its blessed work.

I may be told that all the men whom I have instanced were cast in so great a mould that they cannot fitly be used as examples for common life.

It was to nature, it will be said, not to the accidents of their training that their greatness was due. Johnson, however, was not, I think, far wrong when he maintained that, "the true genius is a mind of large, general powers, accidentally determined to some particular direction." [1] Unless liberty is given, a determining accident may never occur, and the genius may never be unfolded. The poet, as he surveyed the country churchyard, mourned over the waste of intellect:

> " Perhaps in this neglected spot is laid
> Some heart once pregnant with celestial fire ;
> Hands, that the rod of empire might have swayed,
> Or waked to ecstasy the living lyre."

There is a passage in Carlyle's "Life of his Father" which moved some of the critics to scorn, but which seemed to me not unreasonable. " I know Robert Burns," he writes ; " and I knew my father. Yet were you to ask me which had the greater natural faculty, I might perhaps actually pause before replying." He goes on to say : " My father's education was altogether of the worst and most limited. I believe he was never more than three months at any school. What he learned there showed what he might have learned. . . .

[1] Boswell's " Life of Johnson," ii. 437, *n.* 2.

Poetry, fiction in general, he had universally seen treated not only as idle, but false and criminal. . . . Oh ! when I think that all the area in boundless space he had seen was limited to a circle of some fifty miles diameter, and all his knowledge of the boundless time was derived from his Bible and what the oral memories of old men could give him, and his own could gather, and yet that he was such, I could take shame to myself. I feel to my father—so great, though so neglected, so generous also towards *me*—a strange tenderness, and mingled pity and reverence peculiar to the case, infinitely soft and near my heart. Was he not a sacrifice to me ? Had I stood in his place could he not have stood in mine, and more ? "

I see nothing absurd in all this. James Carlyle's natural faculty might well not have been inferior even to that of Burns. He had the gift of eloquence. " None of us," says his son, " will ever forget that bold, glowing style of his, flowing free from his untutored soul, full of metaphors (though he knew not what a metaphor was), with all manner of potent words, which he appropriated and applied with a surprising accuracy." Had the right accident determined his " large general powers," it might have been of books which he had written, not of houses and bridges which he had built, that

his son was to say that "nothing that he undertook
to do, but he did it faithfully and like a true man." [1]
There is, I believe, the same number of good
brains born into the world in every generation,
and of the same quality, too. Every age might
be Elizabethan, were the children who belonged to
it equally favoured by their surroundings. But the
world, I fear, can never again witness that mighty
outburst of noble curiosity which followed on the
discovery of the New World, the translation of
the Bible, and of the great master-pieces of Greece
and Rome. As we look back upon that marvellous
age we may exclaim in Milton's noble words :
" Methinks I see in my mind a noble and puissant
nation rousing herself like a strong man after sleep,
and shaking her invincible locks ; methinks I see
her as an eagle muing her mighty youth, and
kindling her undazzled eyes at the full mid-day
beam ; purging and unscaling her long-abused
sight at the fountain itself of heavenly radiance." [2]
Each generation may, if it choose, rouse itself also.
The fountain of heavenly radiance never ceases to
flow.

> " Labitur et labetur in omne volubilis ævum."
> (" It runs and as it runs, for ever shall run on.")

---

[1] " Reminiscences," i. 8, 18–20.
[2] Milton's "Works," ed. 1806, i. 324.

Thither let us repair, and at its living waters
purge and unscale our long-abused sight. If no
Golden Age of Literature can ever return, we shall
yet be gladdened by one of those Silver Ages,
which till late years almost in unbroken succession
had followed one upon the other. What clusters
of famous writers has our country seen, drawn
together, too, from a far smaller population! Look
at the age of Anne, when there were not perhaps
in the whole of England more people than are now
living in London and its suburbs. Yet "these few,
these happy few" could boast of Defoe, Swift,
Addison, Pope, Steele, Congreve, Prior, Gay,
Arbuthnot, and Burnet. The last years of George
II., that German king of ours, "who cared neither
for Boets nor Bainters," and the first years of his
grandson, who gloried in the name of Briton, and
who set up as a patron of learning, are adorned by
the names of Richardson, Fielding, Smollett, Sterne,
Johnson, Hume, Gray, Collins, Goldsmith, Young,
Burke, Bolingbroke, Horace Walpole, Adam Smith,
and Blackstone. How bright are the opening years
of the present century—a brightness still more dazzling to us who are surrounded by the gloom of its
close! What "radiant files" ushered it in—Scott,
Wordsworth, Coleridge, Campbell, Southey, Rogers,
Lamb, Hazlitt, Cobbett, Jeffrey, Sydney Smith,

Maria Edgeworth, Jane Austen ; and then following close behind them Byron, Shelley, Keats,
Landor, Moore, Leigh Hunt, and De Quincey !
When we set our writers against the writers of the
least favoured of these generations how mean and
and beggarly is the show we make !

> " Though fallen on evil days,
> On evil days though fallen and *evil tongues*,"

we may bring back good days when tongues shall
once more speak as they spoke of yore, if only we
give imagination free play.   Children of the finest
natures are indeed rare ; a schoolmaster may easily
pass through a long life of teaching, and not have
the good fortune to come across a single one.
Nevertheless, he may have not a few of those
whom Wordsworth calls " silent poets " — men
" silently enthusiastic, loving all quiet things, and
poets in everything but words."   Such a man was
his sailor brother who was lost with his ship off the
coast of Dorset.

> " But thou a schoolboy, to the sea hadst carried
> Undying recollections !   Nature there
> Was with thee : she who loved us both, she still
> Was with thee, and even so didst thou become
> A *silent* Poet ; from the solitude
> Of the vast sea didst bring a watchful heart

Still couchant, an inevitable ear,
And an eye practised like a blind man's touch."[1]

We can nurse, and even implant, that love of reading which more than any institution or law sweeps away the inequalities of rank and fortune. "There is," it was finely said of old, "there is as much difference between the learned and the unlearned as between the living and the dead." Your secondhand bookstall is a great leveller of all distinctions. Learning has a prescriptive right to go ragged. It is one of the prerogatives of a scholar to wear an old coat. For a few pence well laid out every week we can live in the best of all company—among the finest and truest gentlemen the world has ever seen. When they come and sit with us by our fireside—Don Quixote, Sir Roger de Coverley, my Uncle Toby, Parson Adams, the Vicar of Wakefield—we can look down with quiet pity on those unfortunate people who, for want of higher and better society, are reduced to playing at baccarat with princes. Our carpet may be ragged, our floor may even be bare of carpet, our chairs may be of the hardest, and our fare of the plainest, they will not be scorned by the fine gentlemen whom we have invited. Draw the curtain, trim the lamp, put a fresh lump of coal on

[1] Wordsworth's " Life," i. 288 ; "Works," i. 355.

the fire, and then call in the goodly company. There they stand waiting at your call with Shakespeare, Milton, Scott, and a host of others ready to usher them in. Farewell, outside world, with your troubles and meanness, your brawls and strife, your hard struggles and petty cares, your din of politics, and your low mutterings of vast changes in the very. fabric of society ; farewell Tories, Liberals, Radicals, Socialists ; farewell Church and Dissent ; welcome thou world of history and of fancy ! Thy fabric may be baseless, thy pageant insubstantial ; thy actors, we shall soon have to own, are

> " All spirits, and
> Are melted into air, into thin air,"

yet while thou dost last, and they throng thy roomy stage, the "radiant courts" of kings and emperors have no more "majestic vision " than that which fills our little parlour. In the palace of King Alcinous a blind minstrel sang to the company as they feasted. " The Muse," says Homer, " loved him dearly, and she gave him both good and evil ; of his sight she bereft him, but granted him sweet song." Those who seek her the Muse loves still—"the silent poets " no less than those who have utterance. Of much we may have been bereft, but the solace of sweet song she freely gives. By her we are

> " taught to live
> The easiest way ; nor with perplexing thoughts
> To interrupt the sweet of life."

There are, however, minds of no low order which find little pleasure in the study of the past, and which turn with indifference from the great works of imagination. Whether any one who has a soul above that of an oyster is naturally indifferent to such subjects I greatly doubt. I never yet came across an intelligent child who did not delight in listening to fairy stories. Nevertheless, whether it comes about by nature or by stupid teaching, even at a somewhat early age this indifference is manifested. The great Darwin who, as I have shown, in his boyhood had delighted in Shakespeare, after the age of thirty could no longer find the slightest enjoyment in the mighty poet, though to the end of his life he could read novels, silly novels, too, if only they ended happily. He mourned over his mental atrophy, as he called it, but he could not overcome it. This atrophy often manifests itself at an early age. Many a man famous in science had been pronounced a blockhead at school, to the lasting disgrace of his teacher, who had failed to discover his genius, or even worse, who had for the time stifled its flame. In that criticism of Milton's scheme of education which I read to you in my last lecture, natures such as these, if they were known to Johnson, were treated by him with neglect. Poets, orators, and historians, you will remember, were to form the sole reading of schoolboys, because they would supply them with axioms of prudence, principles of moral truth, and materials of conversation. The only result of forcing authors such as these on those to whom they are utterly distasteful is far too often to render the unwilling students imprudent, immoral, and dull. Finding no pleasure in the only knowledge which is given them they look upon all knowledge as wearisome. Had they been allowed to do what Johnson seems to despise, "to watch the growth of plants or the motions of the stars," they would have far better learnt that lesson which in Socrates' opinion was what we had to learn—" how to do good and avoid evil." " Whatever," said Johnson, speaking of his visit to the ruins of Iona, "whatever withdraws us from the power of our senses, whatever makes the past, the distant, or the future predominate over the present, advances us in the dignity of thinking beings. Far from me and from my friends be such frigid philosophy as may

conduct us indifferent or unmoved over any ground
which has been dignified by wisdom, bravery, or
virtue. That man is little to be envied whose
patriotism would not gain force upon the plain of
Marathon, or whose piety would not grow warmer
among the ruins of Iona."

But we may be withdrawn from the power of our
senses by other studies than those which deal with
the character of man. To the geologist the past
speaks in tones scarcely less deep and solemn than
to the student of history ; to the naturalist in his
study, as the endless tribes of living things in all
their variety and beauty "flash upon his inward
eye," the distant seems close at hand ; he is making
his way through the forests of the tropics, or sail-
ing among the islands of the East ; while to the
astronomer, as he considers that the earth is slowly
but surely slackening her daily course, till the day
must come when

> " the great globe itself
> Yea all which it inherit shall dissolve
> And . . .
> Leave not a rack behind,"

the future must with sadness often predominate
over the present.

Without the study of our great writers—our

poets, philosophers, historians, biographers, and moralists—I do not think that the full wisdom ot life can be attained. But if we cannot have the best, let us go to the second best, or even to the third best. Let us not be content till we have implanted in every child a love of something that can withdraw him from the power of his senses. He who can succeed in doing this, he who can give the imagination strength and depth and purity, may hope that, as the years go on, those who have come under his happy influence, as each one finds

"from day to day his little boat
Rock in its harbour, lodging peaceably,"

will give each his blessing and his praise to that wise teacher

" Who gave him nobler loves and nobler cares.'

INDEX.

14